PRIZE-WINNING RECIPES FOR HOMEMADE WINES

PRIZE-WINNING RECIPES FOR HOMEMADE WINES

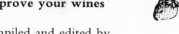

with a review of techniques to help
improve your wines

Compiled and edited by
Rodney Boothroyd

Allison & Busby
Published by W. H. Allen & Co Plc

An Allison & Busby book
Published in 1989 by
W. H. Allen & Co. Plc
Sekforde House
175/9 St John Street
London EC1V 4LL

First published in hardback by Allison & Busby in 1987

Printed in Great Britain
by Cox & Wyman Ltd, Reading, Berkshire

ISBN 0 85031 811 4

Contents

Introduction

The idea for this book was born from a discussion on how home winemakers could achieve better wines. We all agreed that having a set of recipes which had consistently produced successful wines would be very helpful for most winemakers, and that if these recipes were combined with a review of the techniques used by competition winners, the outcome would be a practical handbook of solid worth. So here it is: a guide to wines which have won prizes, produced in the hope that everyone, whether or not they are interested in shows and competitions, will find the book not only useful and interesting, but also a means by which they can improve the quality of their wines, and thereby gain even more enjoyment from this most fascinating hobby.

This book has been put together with both the experienced and novice winemaker in mind. It is not, however, a basic introduction for someone who knows nothing about the subject. If you would like more information on any aspect of winemaking, you will find all the details you need in my previous book *Home Winemaking Techniques and Recipes*.

As you will see, the recipes included in this volume are for wines that have achieved success at local, regional or national shows or competitions in recent years. In many cases, the wine produced from a particular recipe has achieved many more awards than the one I have shown here — I hope the wine-makers concerned do not feel they have thereby been deprived of the recognition they deserve! Although most of the recipes are attributed to their creators, some contributors preferred to remain anonymous, and I have respected their wishes accordingly. Finally, my thanks are due to everyone who submitted recipes, and to all those who otherwise helped in the preparation of this book.

Rodney Boothroyd

PART I

Successful Winemaking

In winemaking, as in cookery, a good recipe isn't everything — although it certainly makes a big difference to your chances of success. This is particularly true of the recipes here, for they have all proved themselves in one way or another. You may well ask if this means that simply following the recipe is a guarantee of success. The answer, of course, is "*No*." You only need to consider the difference in quality of different batches of fruit to realize why this is so. Although two batches may look similar, they can vary considerably in ripeness and flavour: so that if one winemaker compounds a prizewinning wine recipe from a particular batch of ingredients, next time the same recipe may produce what is simply a pleasant wine rather than a potential prizewinner.

When you consider how many other variables play their part in winemaking — the speed of fermentation, for example, or the type of yeast used, or the speed with which a fermented wine is siphoned off the sediment, or the time a wine is allowed to mature — you begin to realize just why so many wines are made and so few win prizes! Even so, the great majority of home winemakers would probably like to improve their standards, yet cannot be bothered with measuring acidity, or

carefully compounding the "must" to precise chemical specifi-
cations. It is here that this book will be at its most valuable,
for each "prizewinning" recipe has achieved, either by luck or
by design, a combination of ingredients which significantly
increases one's chances of successful winemaking.

In addition, some interesting points of technique have
emerged from the prizewinning wine recipes. I have set these
out below in an order which roughly corresponds to the stages
involved in winemaking: extraction of flavour, fermentation,
and maturation. Since the ingredients are what gives home-
made wine its basic character, this is obviously the place to
start.

Fresh fruit

How much simpler it would be if winemaking were just a
matter of extracting the flavour! The problem is that our basic
ingredients usually need some preparation to ensure they are
clean and unlikely to infect the must with bacteria or spoilage
yeasts. You can see how this might happen if you think of the
outer skin of a plum, damson or grape. The "bloom" you see
there is actually a growth of wild yeasts, most of which would
probably be unable to produce very much alcohol, and all of
which would certainly produce curious "off flavours" during
fermentation as by-products of their metabolism (the true wine
yeast has been specially selected so that it does not do this). If
these yeasts are not inactivated before the fruit is added to the
must, they can spoil a fermentation completely.

Similarly, any small cut or bruise on a fruit rapidly becomes
infected with moulds or bacteria: these, too, can ruin a wine.
Clearly any soft or damaged fruit will present a greater risk
of this kind of infection than firm, ripe, fresh fruit (although
soft or over-ripe fruit can still be used if it is sterilized — see
below). Curiously enough, some of these bacterial off-flavours
do not develop until the wine has been stored for some time.

For example, in one case a gallon of raspberry wine made from fresh fruit tasted absolutely delicious after it was racked off the sediment, but four months later it had turned to vinegar — despite the precaution of adding two Campden tablets to the cold pulp must twenty-four hours before adding the yeast. Of course it is possible the infection occurred later during racking, but raspberries in particular do have a reputation for this kind of problem.

Many off-flavours in wine probably result from this kind of infection. What, then, can one do about it? The first answer is to use sound, good quality ripe fruit (except possibly when you are making gooseberry wine, for gooseberries are often said to give a better result if they are used while still hard and green, in other words when they are slightly less than ripe). If necessary, the fruit can be washed in warm water to remove any dust or dirt. Spoilage organisms can then be inhibited by the addition of sodium metabisulphite at the rate of fifty or a hundred parts per million, that is one or two crushed Campden tablets per gallon (4.5 litres); and twenty-four hours later, the yeast can be added. This delay is necessary to allow the sulphite to disperse to a level at which its bactericidal properties will not inhibit the wine yeast.

Unfortunately, sulphite added in this way does not kill all the spoilage organisms in a must: it simply inhibits them so that the yeast can get an upper hand. If you use sulphite as a way of cleaning the must, it is essential to add a vigorous yeast preparation so that there is the minimum delay before the fermentation begins: any delay might allow the spoilage bacteria to recover. These spoilage organisms are further inhibited by the anaerobic conditions which soon prevail as the yeast begins to work. Even so, it seems fairly probable that at least some bacteria may survive right through the fermentation and subsequently spoil the wine, even if a Campden tablet is added when the wine is racked off the sediment. Certainly this would help explain why so many winemakers prefer to sterilize their musts completely with boiling water. In the recipes examined for this book, the use of boiling water was three times more popular than the use of Campden tablets in preparing a must for pulp fermentation!

The objection has been raised that the use of boiling water can produce a "cooked" flavour. I don't agree. Admittedly the flavour of some ingredients may be slightly altered by the use of boiling water (and even that is open to question in many cases), but this does not necessarily mean that the flavour thus obtained is inferior: in fact the opposite is often true. One only has to think of the intense concentration of flavour in canned fruits (all of which are cooked) and compare it with the weak flavour of so many modern fresh fruits to realize that heating can indeed aid the winemaker. This is particularly true where commercial pressures lead growers to select varieties on the basis of yield rather than flavour. However, one thing is certain; if you want to sterilize a must made from fresh fruit, you will have to use either boiling water or a steam juice extractor, or boil the fruit.

We can obtain more information about the relative advantages of hot and cold water preparation by looking at the techniques used in commercial wineries, many of which have taken the idea of heat treatment a step further. In some French co-operatives, and in many Australian, South African and Californian vineyards, red grapes are placed in steam or hot water for a few minutes so that the surface of the fruit is heated. The grapes are then cooled and pressed, and the resulting juice — which is a deep red colour — is fermented directly, without any pulp whatsoever. This is quite contrary to the traditional practice of fermenting red wine musts on the pulp to extract both colour and tannin from the fruit skins. Yet it has been claimed that this newer method can produce softer, less acidic wines with a better bouquet and greater fullness; and that the practice is not more widespread simply because of the expense involved.

Now, if these claims are correct, it follows that home wine-makers might be able to improve the quality of wine made from elderberries, plums, damsons, blackberries and black grapes by adapting the technique to their own use. The late Ben Turner, who was one of the foremost experts on home winemaking, suggested that this could be done by heating these fruits in water to a temperature of 60–80°C (140–176°F) for about twenty minutes before pressing the fruit pulp to extract the juice and then fermenting it directly in a demijohn under air-lock. I have tried this myself on a small scale, and it seems to work quite well; it is interesting to see that several of the prizewinning recipes for elderberry wine included in this book use a similar technique.

While on the subject of elderberries, it is worth mentioning that prizewinning elderberry wines are made in a great variety of ways. These include:

(i)   the use of canned elderberry juice
(ii) the fermentation of juice extracted
(iii) the use of a steam juice extractor
(iv) pulp fermentation

This might mean that the key to success lies more in the quality of elderberry used than the method employed. (However, the maturation time is undoubtedly important as well. This is because these wines do need time to mature, particularly if they are fermented on the pulp, a procedure which can extract a considerable amount of tannin from the fruit.) So try to ensure, as for any wine, that the berries are ripe, fat and juicy. It is a good idea to taste a few from each tree before you pick them. The ones best suited to winemaking have little or no apparent flavour when eaten raw; certainly you should avoid any which taste bitter or woody.

Similarly, blackberries, bilberries and damsons should be at their peak: ripe but firm, sweet and not too acid. Of course it isn't always easy to obtain ripe fruit in an English summer or autumn. If you have to use fruit which is sour and acidic, it is a good idea to heat it almost to boiling point in water and maintain the temperature for a few minutes. (You may prefer to do this anyway.) Bottled bilberries are a superb winemaking ingredient, but they are rather hard to find. At the time of writing, one frozen-food chain has a plan to import frozen Canadian blueberries. If the plan ever comes to fruition, this would be a good substitute.

One fruit which seems to represent an exception to the rule of scrupulous care always being necessary in the preparation of ingredients is the apple. Several winemakers have reported that clean, sound apples will produce a good wine if the pulp, or the juice extracted from the pulp, is protected simply by Campden tablets. In fact commercial cidermakers simply wash, chop and press their apples before directly fermenting the extracted juice, a procedure which implies that any Campden tablets added by the home winemaker serve to prevent the fruit from browning rather than to protect it against infection. (Browning is an oxidation reaction which can ruin the taste and appearance of a wine. The enzymes responsible for browning — and this applies to all fruits, it is simply more noticeable with apples — are destroyed by boiling, another fact which may help explain why boiling water is so popular in the preparation of home-made wines.)

One important point which has not been generally reco-gnized relates to citrus fruits. Oranges, grapefruits and other citrus fruits are lightly coated with an organic chemical preservative which can sometimes be seen on the fruit as a white powdery deposit. This preservative should be washed off the fruit before the rind is used as an ingredient. Of course it presents no problem if the juice is being extracted from the fruits, so long as the juice is run off into the must without coming into contact with the fruit skins.

You may be surprised at how often bananas feature as an ingredient in the prizewinning wine recipes. They are actually used to improve the body of a wine. The bananas are usually peeled, sliced and boiled in water for a few minutes before the resulting "juice" is strained off and added to the must. Although the boiling produces a pungent aroma, the liquid can be safely added to a must without fear of it affecting the bouquet and flavour produced by the main ingredients. The banana skins are best discarded, since they can contribute an excessively strong flavour.

Turning back to more general points, many winemakers have suggested that using frozen fruit helps to extract the flavour. Certainly this seems reasonable, since freezing ruptures the fruit tissue and allows the contents of the cells to escape more easily when the fruit is subsequently thawed. In some cases this may add to the fruitiness of the finished wine, and it seems to be a technique well worth experimenting with.

Another idea which features quite often in the prizewinning wine recipes is the addition of Bentonite (a wine-clearing agent made from clay) at the start of fermentation, or when the must is compounded. On the face of it this seems difficult to understand. How can adding Bentonite to a wine must improve the finished wine? Perhaps we can obtain some guidance on this question from an article entitled "A Bentonite Experiment" which appeared in the December 1976 issued of the *Amateur Winemaker* magazine (now called *Winemaker and Brewer*).

Following an observation that French wine producers sometimes add Bentonite to their wine musts, Derek Fraser conducted an experiment to investigate the effects of adding Bentonite to an apple-based must. He discovered that adding Bentonite at the rate of 5 grams to the gallon (4.5 litres) produced a superior wine with a paler colour and a better bouquet. This effect appears to be due partly to the fact that Bentonite can precipitate proteins out of suspension, and partly to the fact that it helps the wine clear faster after fermentation.

The Gervin winemaking supplies company run by Professor

Gerry Fowles produces two brands of Bentonite which have been specially developed for adding to a must as well as for clearing wine after fermentation. They absorb water easily, so a brief soaking, rather than the twenty-four hours usually recommended, is all that is needed before the Bentonite is added to the must. These preparations are said to remove undesirable compounds which could leave a musty taste, and also to ensure a smoother fermentation, a clearer wine, and an absence of yeasty off-flavours. If you should try the idea of adding Bentonite, always soak the dry Bentonite powder in water in accordance with the instructions before you use it, or alternatively use the premixed Bentonite gel which comes in sealed sachets.

Incidentally, Mr Fraser discovered in his experiment that the "superior" wine did not clear properly later on — undoubtedly because the Bentonite had precipitated not only unwanted proteins in the must but also the pectic enzyme added at the start. (Pectic enzyme is itself a protein compound.) In other words, adding Bentonite may help to improve a wine's quality, but does so at the risk of making it cloudy. So if you feel the potential improvement in quality justifies the addition of Bentonite, you would be wise to delay adding it until two days or so after the pectic enzyme has been added, regardless of when you add the yeast.

Dried and canned fruit

Dried fruit is a useful and popular winemaking ingredient. Weight for weight, one pound (450 grams) of dried fruit is roughly equal to four pounds (1.8 kilograms) of fresh fruit, although this is only an approximate guide. In some cases quite a high proportion of the weight of the dried fruit is sugar: one pound (450 grams) of raisins, for example, may contain up to 50% or more sugar. Although some of this sugar is probably not available to the yeast, being chemically bound up with the fruit tissue, the sugar content of dried fruit should be borne in mind if you are formulating your own recipes.

Dried fruit is by no means sterile. It should be chopped and soaked overnight in water with a Campden tablet, or simmered for a few minutes in boiling water before use. Many white or golden dried fruits are coated with sulphite as a preservative; this not only inhibits the action of spoilage bacteria but also prevents the fruit from browning. For example, dried apricots come in all shades between yellow and brown. The yellow ones have much more sulphite on them than the brown ones, and they therefore need to be simmered in boiling water for about fifteen or twenty minutes to drive off the preservative. This will ensure that the yeast is not inhibited during the early stages of fermentation.

Raisins, currants and sultanas are all packed in food-grade mineral oil to keep them shiny and prevent them sticking together during storage. For the winemaker, this oil is a real nuisance, for if it is not carefully washed off with hot water, it can float on top of the must and the wine, looking most unappealing and possibly even inhibiting the yeast by cutting off its oxygen supply. It isn't easy to remove, either, and several washes in hot water may be required. You should do this before chopping or mincing the fruit, whether or not the recipe using these fruits mentions the fact.

Canned fruit is sterile and can be added directly to the must without need of either Campden tablets or hot water. However, it is a good idea to assess the amount of sugar in the syruped variety by using a hydrometer if you have one, although this is not essential.

Flowers and grain

Some delightful wines can be made using fresh or dried flowers, but it is best to be a little cautious about the preparation of the must. Fresh flowers seem to withstand the addition of boiling water better than dried ones; indeed, some dried flowers are totally ruined by this procedure. It has to be admitted, however, that the use of boiling water on dried elderflowers seems to be quite a common practice.

Even so, I would suggest that the character of flower wines can best be preserved by infusing the flowers in water at about 60°C (140°F) — the temperature of hot tea — and then adding the liquid to the fermenting must. Nevertheless, you will see that many of the prizewinning wine recipes for flower wines in this book specify the use of boiling water, so clearly the outcome of this technique depends more on the nature of the individual ingredients than on a general principle.

An alternative approach to the preparation of flower wines is to suspend the dried flowers in a small muslin or nylon mesh bag inside a demijohn of fermenting must for a few days. Several experts think it is better to do this after the first vigorous fermentation has died down, on the grounds that the volatile oils and esters responsible for the flowery bouquet may be driven off by the force of carbon dioxide leaving the surface of the fermenting liquid during the initial stages of fermentation.

Very often, elderflowers or rose petals are included in a wine to enhance the bouquet. If you use fresh elderflowers for this purpose, you should test the scent of the flowers before you pick them: as a general rule, the best flowers are white or cream in colour. As a bonus, you will probably find that the trees which have the most pleasant flowers also have the best berries in the autumn, a fact which may help you improve your elderberry wine! If you use dried flowers you are in the hands of the suppliers, although the quality is generally satisfactory.

Vegetables and cereals

All vegetable wines are prepared in the same way: the clean vegetables are diced or chopped, boiled in unsalted water and then strained off. Only the liquor is used to compound the must. The same guidelines apply to fresh fruit: that is to say, you should choose the best and reject out of hand any which are mouldy or unsound.

Cereals should be washed to remove dust or dirt before use, and the inclusion of the recommended dose of an amylase enzyme preparation (which destroys starch) will prevent any starch haze in the finished wine. This is also true of vegetable wines.

Sugar

Ordinary white granulated sugar is excellent for winemaking, but whenever it is added to a must or wine it should be completely dissolved and mixed into the bulk of the liquid. This is because any yeast which is subjected to too high a sugar concentration is either inhibited or killed; and this can happen easily enough if sugar or sugar syrup are added to a wine and not mixed in properly. The sugar will sink to the bottom of the vessel, form a thick, dense layer on top of the yeast, and stop it working. The question of how much sugar to use, and how it should be added, is dealt with in detail later on.

As you may know, before yeast can ferment granulated sugar (chemically known as sucrose) to alcohol, it has to "invert" or split the sucrose molecule into two simpler sugars known as glucose and fructose:

$$C_{12}H_{22}O_{11}+H_2O \rightarrow C_6H_{12}O_6+C_6H_{12}O_6$$

$$\text{Sucrose} \rightarrow \text{Glucose} + \text{Fructose}$$

Therefore, you might think that it would be possible to "help" the yeast, so to speak, by inverting the sugar in advance. (This is a simple enough process; one just boils the sugar in water with a little citric acid for a few minutes.) In reality, inverting the sugar is not necessary; the yeast has all the enzymes necessary to complete the transformation, and inverting the sugar in advance will neither effect a significantly faster fermentation nor produce a stronger one. (It follows that purchasing glucose and fructose is simply an unnecessary expense.) However it is only fair to point out that although inverting the sugar may not do any good, it certainly won't do any harm either!

Other forms of sugar can be used. Soft brown sugar has sometimes been suggested for robust red wines or sherries, on the basis that it contains a proportion of molasses which, although entirely fermentable, does add a certain extra character to the flavour of the wine. Golden syrup has success-fully been included in recipes for several types of wine. Although its flavour is distinctive and may be out of place in a delicate table wine or aperitif, I think it can add a certain extra character to the right sort of must. It contains about 80% sugar by weight, 17% water, 1.5% minerals, and 1.5% non-sugar organic matter. It is the last two ingredients which are responsible for the characteristic flavour of syrup. If you like to use invert sugar, you will be delighted to learn that golden syrup contains 66% glucose and fructose. On a weight for weight basis, one pound (450 grams) of golden syrup is equi-valent to about thirteen ounces (368 grams) of sucrose.

Honey can of course be used for sweetening, and is the basic ingredient in mead. However, unless it is pasteurized before bottling, and is therefore sterile, it will contain many micro-organisms and bacteria, and will need to be boiled in water before being added to the must or wine.

Yeast and nutrients

Of all the variety of ingredients available to the home wine-maker, possibly more importance has been attached to the yeast than to any other single factor. This is not surprising, for the entire fermentation depends on it. Broadly speaking, our wine yeasts are derived from carefully selected and cultured yeasts growing naturally on grapes. There are four characteristics common to all true wine yeasts:

(i) they ferment quickly
(ii) they produce relatively high levels of alcohol
(iii) they settle out quickly when fermentation is complete
(iv) they tend not to produce off-flavours in the finished wine.

Any good wine yeast will produce a successful fermentation on that basis: these are the yeasts known as "general-purpose" or "all-purpose" varieties. But there are also specific varieties of yeast available to the home winemaker such as those labelled Bordeaux, Burgundy, Chablis, Madeira, Port and Sauternes. These are particular strains of yeast derived from yeasts which have been selected (by nature or by man) to ferment particular types of grape in different winemaking regions of the world. For example, a Sauternes yeast can tolerate the high levels of sugar typically found in a Sauternes must, and it also produces a great deal of glycerol during fermentation: the glycerol being a distinctive feature of the rich, sweet Sauternes.

In theory, the use of a specific variety of yeast can help to develop characteristics of bouquet and flavour in a home-made wine reminiscent of those found in the corresponding type of commercial wine — provided that the composition of the must has some similarity to the type of grape must for which the yeast was originally developed. You can demonstrate the different properties of these various strains of yeast by fermenting two identical musts with different yeasts: you may well find that the finished wines do indeed have slightly different bouquets and flavours.

Where a specific variety of yeast has been used in a recipe for a prizewinning wine, that fact is recorded. Obviously you could substitute a good general-purpose yeast if you wanted.

Most types of yeast, whether general-purpose or for specific use, come as dried cultures in sealed packets. (Liquid cultures on agar jelly are also available.) In such packets you may well find that the manufacturers have economized on the quantity of yeast by "diluting" it with nutrient salts. This means that the amount of yeast in a packet is so small that it cannot be added directly to the must: if you were to do so, the yeast would take so long to establish a vigorous colony that the risk of bacterial infection would be significantly increased. To avoid this problem, the yeast is first reconstituted in a "starter" bottle and allowed to establish a strong, vigorous colony before it is added to the must. Although it is not difficult to prepare a starter bottle, you should do it carefully, since the success of the entire fermentation may depend on the vigour of the yeast colony established at this stage.

The simplest way of preparing a yeast starter is to mix the yeast with about half a pint (300 ml) of tepid water in a sterile glass bottle or jar, together with a tablespoonful of sugar, a little acid and some nutrient. These quantities should be deducted from the amounts specified in the recipe. (Orange juice and malt extract are often included in a starter bottle because they provide acid and nutrients for the yeast: see, for example, Mr Michael Dickinson's recipe for Sultana and Raisin Wine.) Once mixed, the culture should be left in a warm place at about 25°C (75°F) for at least several hours. If you have bought a packet which contains very little yeast, you may need to leave the starter for up to forty-eight hours before adding it to the must. The neck of the jar should be plugged with cotton wool or the top lightly screwed on during this time.

Among the recipes for prizewinning wines reproduced in this book, the Gervin brand yeasts feature quite prominently. There are seven types of yeast available in the range, each of which has been selected for a different purpose. For example, Number 3 is a yeast selected for its ability to tolerate high levels of both sugar and alcohol: it is therefore good at restarting stuck fermentations. The Red Circle variety is a French yeast from Bordeaux used for making claret-style wines. It is described by the French producers as "an aromatic yeast which develops a pleasant and lasting aroma". It quickly starts to ferment with minimum frothing and has a high sugar to alcohol conversion rate. It is also claimed to produce a good yield of glycerol. To take a final example, Number 4 is a Californian sherry flor yeast which will carry out the secondary fermentation of base wines with 12–15% alcohol, and produce the aldehyde levels required for a true sherry nose and taste. (This procedure is discussed in detail in the sherry recipes in Part II.) All the Gervin yeasts are packed in triple foil nitrogen-filled sachets. One plus point, in my opinion, is that these yeasts are not diluted with nutrient salts; they therefore need little preparation time before being added to the must.

Incidentally, if you wish to prepare a wine high in alcohol, the Madeira and Tokay strains of yeast are generally accepted as having a high tolerance of alcohol, although good reports have also been received of CWE's Formula 67 in this respect and no doubt other varieties will work well too. For the production of sherry, a good sherry flor yeast is vital.

You will see that all the prizewinning wine recipes specify yeast nutrient as an ingredient, a fact which emphasizes the importance of these preparations in obtaining a good fermentation. Ammonium phosphate and sulphate are the nutrients commonly recommended, for they provide the chemicals needed by the yeast in the intermediate stages of the metabolic conversion of sugar to alcohol. It is also a good idea, particularly if you are making a wine of high alcoholic content, to add a vitamin B^1 supplement to ensure that the yeast has the best possible environment.

Vitamin B^1 is available in three-milligram tablets under various brand names from both chemists and winemaking shops. Try to avoid tablets which are strongly coloured and flavoured, since this might affect the taste of the wine. Neutral tablets sold under the chemical name of thiamin or aneurin hydrochloride are available from winemaking shops. Ready prepared vitaminized nutrients, such as Tronozymol or Gervin's Minavit are perhaps a little simpler and more convenient.

Incidentally, yeast nutrient compounds are denatured by hot or boiling water (the ammonium compounds dissociate to produce ammonia, which adds nothing to the flavour of the must!), so do check that the must is cool before the nutrients are added.

Water

There are two distinctly divided schools of thought on whether or not the water used in home winemaking should be boiled. Some winemakers insist on it; others do not bother. Perhaps the first point to bear in mind when considering this question is that for five-gallon (22.5 litre) batches of wine, boiling the water may simply be impractical. But for most home winemakers, who undoubtedly produce smaller quantities of wine, the question "to boil or not to boil" assumes greater importance.

If you live in an area where the tap water is clean, fresh and relatively free from chlorine, you may be content to use water straight from the tap. However, if you face the problem — and it is not at all uncommon — of a water company which supplies you with dull, recycled, deoxygenated water full of chlorine, it is probably better to boil the water before you use it. This will drive off the chlorine, which has otherwise been known to bleach the colour out of the wine as well as ruining the flavour. An alternative procedure is to use a carbon filter which clips onto the tap. This absorbs the chlorine by chemical action and produces a purer water.

One point about boiling is that it displaces any oxygen

dissolved in the water. Since the early stages of growth of a yeast colony depend upon the presence of oxygen, you may therefore find that fermentation in a must prepared with boiled water tends to "stick". One way to overcome this problem is to aerate the boiled water or the must itself by vigorous stirring, or by pouring it from one container to another.

Little, if any, research has been done on the effects of the bacteriological purity and hardness of water on winemaking. Tap water is not necessarily sterile, but it contains no organisms harmful to humans. Any micro-organisms it does contain will probably be of little significance if a vigorous yeast starter is added to the must and fermentation begins straight away. However, added unboiled tap water to top up a demijohn is asking for infection, and I suggest that topping up after racking, for example, be done with cool, boiled water. Of course concentrated or natural strength grape juice can be used if you want to sweeten a wine, and if you have a large airspace to fill. Another possibility would be to use a similar wine for topping up; this would ensure that the flavour, body or strength of your new wine were not diluted.

One or two experts have hinted that very soft water may cause a must to ferment more slowly, possibly owing to a deficiency of certain magnesium salts in the water. I feel this is unlikely to be of any real significance, but the deficiency — if it is such — can be corrected by adding a pinch of Epsom Salts (magnesium sulphate) to the must, and you will see that some prizewinners have specified this in their instructions.

Concentrated grape juice

Nearly all the recipes in this book call for the addition of concentrated grape juice, and those that do not usually require raisins or sultanas. These ingredients are used to provide what is known as vinosity — a true wine character based on the wine's aroma, body and the way it tastes both before and after swallowing. No doubt the grape acids also contribute to a good bouquet and flavour. Try to use a good quality "standard" type concentrate, that is one which needs about ten to twelve ounces (300–350 grams) of extra sugar per gallon (4.5 litres) when made up in its own right, and not the "superior" variety which contains extra sugar.

Incidentally, although the fact may not always have been recorded in the recipes, some contributors did recommend particular makes of concentrated grape juice. Looking through all the recipes submitted for this book I find that 25% of the contributors who used concentrated grape juice in their wines mentioned a particular make. These recommendations were split evenly between CWE and SolVino. Only one other brand was mentioned by name — and that only once! Of course this should not be taken to mean that the quality of other grape concentrates is inferior, but it is interesting.

In my own view, it is best to avoid any white-grape juice concentrates which have a darkish brown tinge — this hints at oxidation. Some wineries prepare their concentrates in an inert atmosphere of nitrogen, which may explain why some white grape juice concentrates are a much lighter yellow colour than others. In addition, I think there is a strong case for manufacturers being much more specific about the nature of the ingredients listed on some cans as "flavouring". We ought to know whether this description merely refers to added fruit juices or if it also includes artificial flavourings. The latter should certainly be avoided at all times.

Acid

Perhaps the major reason why the same recipe can produce a significantly different wine on successive occasions is that the acid content of different batches of fruit is rarely the same. It follows that one of the weakest points in a recipe is the stipulation of a specific quantity of acid, for although this is unlikely to be so far inaccurate that it spoils the wine, the inaccuracy may be sufficient to turn a potential prizewinner into everyday plonk.

Acid is such an important ingredient in wine because it is needed both for the effective action of the yeast and the development of a satisfactory bouquet and taste. It is certainly true that many home-made wines suffer from a lack of acid, yet how many home winemakers have the ability or knowledge to use professional laboratory equipment in a bid to titrate their wines? Exceptionally few, in my experience. This is why most winemakers are content — quite rightly — to follow the recommendations about acid additions provided by someone who has formulated a successful wine recipe. Nevertheless a few general observations about acids may be helpful.

The most commonly known acids are citric, tartaric and malic. The high level of citric acid in citrus fruits certainly explains why those fruits feature as ingredients in recipes for aperitif wines rather than table wines. It also explains why lemon and orange juice were once so popular as ingredients for raising the acidity level of wine musts. Unfortunately citric acid does not contribute very much to the bouquet of a wine, a fact which undoubtedly accounts for the more widespread use of tartaric acid and malic acid (the latter often in the form of apple juice) in the prizewinning recipes in this book.

One advantage of tartaric acid is that any excess may precipitate out as insoluble potassium tartrate during storage, while malic acid seems to produce a fruity freshness in a wine. Perhaps the best compromise is to use a blend of citric, malic and tartaric acids in equal proportions; where "acid blend" is specified in the ingredients, that is what is required. Succinic acid is also widely available, and claims have been put forward about its ability to promote the development of the fragrant chemical compounds known as esters during maturation, so leading to a better bouquet. I feel its value in this context may have been overrated, a view possibly supported by the fact that it didn't feature in a single one of the prizewinning recipes submitted for this book! However, you will see that Mr R. N. Brooksbank has specified both lactic acid and acetic acid in his recipe for Bilberry and Elderberry Dry Red Table Wine, so it seems that these acids *can* be useful in promoting the development of a beautiful range of esters during storage.

Tannin

The home winemaker cannot test a must to ensure the level of tannin it contains is correct: he has to rely on a recipe or on his sense of taste. In red wines, tannin should provide a certain astringency without any unpleasant bitterness or off-taste. It also helps to clear a wine by combining with substances which might otherwise remain in suspension and make the wine hazy. But although it is important to a wine's quality, tannin also increases the length of time needed for a wine to mature and mellow. For example, the elderberry contains a great deal of tannin, and one popular "rule" describes the effect that the extraction of tannin from the fruit during pulp fermentation subsequently has upon the necessary storage time: "Each day on the pulp means a year in the bottle". This relationship probably accounts for the popularity of elderberry wine recipes based on juice rather than pulp fermentation: wines produced using the former method will generally be ready much sooner than those prepared by pulp fermentation.

Most of the prizewinning wine recipes which call for the addition of tannin specify the powdered form, although one or two winemakers use the liquid form. If you find that some of the red wine recipes are a little low in tannin for your taste, the appropriate adjustment can easily be made by adding another quarter or half teaspoon per gallon.

White wines contain much less tannin than red wines — the figures quoted by one authority are 0.05% and 0.2% respectively. In practical terms, the amount of tannin needed to reach this figure varies according to how much is already present in the basic ingredients. Musts which contain no tannin, such as those based on flowers, may require anything up to one teaspoonful. On the other hand, where apples, grape juice, or raisins and sultanas are included in a must, probably little if any extra will be needed. In passing it is interesting to observe that the amount of tannin specified in these prizewinning recipes varies considerably; this variation is difficult to explain but it may be at least partly accounted for by differences in personal taste and judges' standards. To sum up: if you are in any doubt, follow the recipe.

One wine where the tannin content must not be allowed to rise too high is sherry, which generally contains less than 0.01% tannin. Fining with gelatine or isinglass will remove excess tannin, a fact which can be useful in the production of both sherry and red wines; conversely, if you wish to maintain the tannin level of a wine, the best fining agent to use is Bentonite.

Pectic enzyme

Pectic enzyme is essential if a finished wine is to have any chance of clearing properly. This is because the enzyme destroys plant pectins which otherwise remain in suspension and make the wine hazy. Both liquid and powdered pectic enzyme are available under various brand names such as Pecto-lase, Pectinol and Pectolytic Enzyme. Additionally, Rohament P is a useful enzyme which breaks down fruit tissue and thereby releases both flavour and colour; however, it will not on its own produce a clear wine, and it therefore needs to be used in conjunction with a pectic enzyme.

Other additives

There are many other additives available to the home wine-maker, all of which are claimed by the manufacturer to improve the wine in some way. For example, the Gervin company produces an oak extract powder designed for adding to red or dessert wines to produce a mature taste and "mouthfeel". Such products can be useful — see, for example, the comments by Mr R. N. Brooksbank on his use of oak chippings in the preparation of Bilberry and Elderberry Dry Red Table Wine.

One can also purchase red and white wine "improvers": these are concentrated solutions of the esters most commonly found in commercial red and white wines. When such solutions are added to a home-made wine and left for adequate periods to mature and blend in with the chemical structure of the wine, one might expect an improvement in the bouquet. However, there was not one reference to any of these products in the prizewinning wine recipes submitted for this book, so unless winemakers feel that they should keep the use of these products secret (!), it would appear "wine improvers" have not made much impact on the home-winemaking scene. For the moment, then, the value of these compounds remains a matter for individual winemakers to discover through their own experiments.

The final additive worth a mention is one which nearly everyone will be aware of — potassium sorbate (not to be confused with sorbitol, an artificial sweetener). Sorbate is added to stabilize a wine at the rate of one gram per gallon (4.5 litres) together with one Campden tablet per gallon. It is a powerful inhibitor of mould and yeast growth and is therefore useful in stopping fermentation when sugar is still present in the wine (this is discussed in more detail below).

Types of wine

As the recipes in this book are classified by the type of wine they are supposed to produce, some discussion of the different categories of wine and how they are made is in order. The four types of wine can be described as follows:

Aperitif
A wine drunk before a meal to stimulate the appetite.
Table Wine
A wine drunk during a meal. Medium strength bouquet and flavour, usually dry or medium dry with rather less body than a social or dessert wine. Generally 10–12% alcohol by volume.
Social Wine
Intended for drinking at any time other than before, during or after a meal. Has a heavier body and stronger bouquet and flavour than a table wine; usually also stronger and sweeter than a table wine.
Dessert Wine
Drunk with, and after, the sweet and dessert courses of a meal. Has a stronger bouquet and flavour and heavier body than either a table or a social wine. Needs a higher level of alcohol to "carry" its sweetness.

(As far as wine is concerned, body is a difficult word to define. It has been described as "the strength of flavour due to the ingredients used", "the presence of enough fruit and an overall well-balanced drink", and "a combination of strength of flavour, robustness and vinosity". To gain a practical idea of what constitutes body, think of the nature and consistency of a "light" white Italian table wine, a "heavy" red table wine, and a rich, sweet Port.)

The novice winemaker may well ask how one can make a particular type of wine. A little thought reveals that the key factors must be the amount (and nature) of the ingredients, and the levels of sugar and alcohol in the finished wine. As far as the first two factors are concerned, the general rule is that dessert and social wines need more fruit to provide a greater body. Of course this is only a general guide and you will no doubt find some table wine recipes which call for more fruit and grape juice than some dessert wine recipes. This discrepancy is not because of some mistake on the part of the winemaker, but can be explained by factors such as variations in the quality of the fruit used in particular cases. This means that if you ever decide to enter a show you should select the wines you enter by sight and taste rather than by the name of the recipe used. Many wines fail to get prizes because they are in the wrong class.

The sugar and alcohol levels appropriate to finished wines of different types is a rather more tricky question, particularly given the reluctance of many home winemakers to use a hydrometer. Obviously, any sugar which is present in a wine and makes it taste sweet when it is served will either have been added by the winemaker after the wine had fermented to dryness and cleared, or have been left in the wine when the fermentation came to an end.

As far as table wines are concerned, this issue does not often arise, simply because many table wines are dry. If, however, a medium-dry table wine — which many people prefer — is required, the question of which procedure to adopt becomes more important. The simpler procedure is to produce a dry wine of the desired strength, to stabilize it and allow it to clear, and finally to sweeten the wine as required. The danger here is that any active yeast cells which remain in the wine may re-ferment when the sugar is added, thereby blowing out the bottle stoppers and perhaps wasting some wine. One can get round this problem in several ways:

(i) by waiting until the wine is crystal clear and has been racked off all the sediment before sweetening it

(ii) by filtering the wine (this is not recommended since it often seems to have an adverse effect on quality)

(iii) by adding a non-fermentable sugar such as lactose

(iv) by adding an artificial sweetener such as saccharin or one of the new non-sugar sweeteners made from aspartame, such as Canderel or Nutra-Sweet.

The alternative procedure is to stop the fermentation when there is still some sugar left in the wine, so that you end up with a wine of both the desired alcohol level and the desired sweetness. This approach entails using a hydrometer to measure the specific gravity of the wine as fermentation proceeds, but that isn't difficult. (A section on the use of the hydrometer is included as an appendix.) In some cases, this procedure seems to give a better drink than the one obtained by sweetening a dry wine. For example, Dr Philip Dransfield, in his recipe for Summer Fruits Social Wine, mentions that the wine seems to lose fruitiness if it is fermented to dryness and then sweetened, and says he prefers to stop the fermentation while some sugar remains in the wine.

How can this be done? The first point to make is that one cannot kill a vigorous wine yeast by using Campden tablets alone: you would need about eight tablets per gallon to do that, and this level of sulphite would ruin the wine. However, a drop in temperature will help (unless you are using a cold-fermenting yeast), so you could start by moving the wine to a cool place, that is 15°C (60°F) or less. This will inhibit the yeast and encourage it to drop out of suspension to form a sediment. The wine can then be racked off into a clean container with potassium sorbate and one Campden tablet and left to clear completely. One or two more rackings should produce the desired result: a non-dry, stable wine. Fining with Bentonite (or Isinglass in the case of a red wine) will speed up the settling-out of any yeast left in suspension, but filtering is to be avoided if possible since it seems to cause an indefinable loss of quality in a wine.

One point which often confuses beginners is the suggestion that sugar should be added in stages. The idea is to avoid producing a must in which the concentration of sugar is so high that the yeast cannot work effectively. For despite the fact that yeast ferments sugar to alcohol, if the amount of sugar in the must is too great *at any one time* the yeast either works inadequately or not at all and thereby just produces an over-sweet "wine" low in alcohol. This problem generally doesn't arise with table wines, where the total amount of sugar in the must is usually well below the level at which the yeast cannot cope. This means that all the sugar could be added at the start of fermentation, although in practice it is often added in two stages: at the beginning of the pulp fermentation and again when the wine is transferred to a demijohn. The same is true of many social wines.

However, if you were aiming for a strong aperitif or dessert wine (say 15–17% alcohol by volume) and you added all the sugar needed to produce this level of alcohol at the start, it is quite possible that the yeast would only work for a few days and then stop because the osmotic pressure of the sugar was too high for it. This problem can be avoided by adding about half or two thirds of the sugar to start with, and the remainder in four-ounce (110 gram) lots at intervals towards the end of fermentation. You will find a hydrometer useful here, for the usual technique is to dissolve four ounces (110 grams) of sugar or a pint (150 ml) of "standard" sugar syrup (see page 000) in the wine each time the specific gravity drops to 1.010 or less. This will ensure that the yeast is never faced with too much sugar, and even when it has produced the maximum level of alcohol it can tolerate (about 17–18%; anything over that would be exceptional), the sugar which remains in the wine will not make the finished drink too sweet.

If you wanted to produce a strong, dry wine it would be necessary to add the sugar in two-ounce (60 gram) lots each time the specific gravity fell to 1.000. Alternatively, you could watch the rate of fall of the specific gravity as fermentation proceeded; when a stage was reached where the s.g. fell by only 0.001 or 0.002 (or less) each day, you would immediately know that the yeast's activity was coming to an end, and that no more sugar should be added. During this procedure, bear in mind that a dry wine can always be sweetened to taste, but an over-sweet wine can only be redeemed by blending it with a dry one. Therefore, err on the side of caution when you add your sugar.

A beginner may ask, when producing a strong, sweet wine, "Why go to all the trouble of adding sugar in 4-ounce (110 gram) lots? You can add three pounds (1.35 kilograms) of sugar at the start and get a strong wine with sweetness left in it." This is true, but only up to a certain point. First, the yeast may "stick" as described earlier. Secondly, if the must is well-balanced with the correct nutrients and maintained at the optimum temperature, the yeast may just ferment out all the sugar and produce a strong dry wine which then needs sweetening; on the other hand it may produce a weak, over-sweet wine — you cannot be certain beforehand.

But what about those winemakers who are reluctant to use a hydrometer? My advice to anyone who feels this way and wants to produce a strong, sweet wine would be to adopt the following compromise: use a total of three pounds (1.35 kilograms) of sugar added in two stages — remembering that one pint (550 ml) of grape concentrate contains roughly one pound (450 grams) of sugar — and let the wine ferment as far as it will go. You can then sweeten to taste. But even this technique leaves room for error: if there is a high amount of sugar naturally present in the fruit, the yeast may still be faced with too high a level of sugar.

Sweetening

Many winemakers find it helpful to have a guide to the average specific gravities and sugar contents of wines in various classes. As a rough guide, the final specific gravities of wines fall into the ranges listed below. These figures apply whether the final product is obtained by sweetening a dry wine or by stopping a fermentation:

Dry 0.980–1.000   Medium 0.995–1.005   Sweet 1.005–1.020

In point of fact, a "dry" wine may actually contain a trace of sugar; indeed, a totally sugar-free wine often tastes very harsh. The categories overlap because the specific gravity of a wine is affected by factors other than the sugar content: in particular, the wine's body and its level of alcohol. Furthermore, since a judge assesses a wine's quality by taste and not with a hydrometer, that is how the home winemaker should do so too.

The table below serves as a general guide to the amount of sugar one would expect to find in wines of different types. However, individual taste is the factor of overriding importance, and you may find, for example, that the figures quoted for "sweet" wines produce a wine just a little too sweet for your palate. Therefore, when you are sweetening a wine to taste, always add the sugar a little at a time, mixing well and tasting carefully after each addition. If your palate becomes jaded, you will probably find it better to come back to the task the next day.

Many winemakers prefer to add sugar as a syrup, for this avoids the problem of dissolving the sugar in the wine and makes the mixing much easier. If you use a sugar syrup you may find the following information helpful:

(i) One pound (450 grams) of sugar dissolved in half a pint (285 ml) of boiling water and then allowed to cool will produce one pint (570 ml) of "standard" sugar syrup. A quarter of a pint of this standard syrup contains four ounces of sugar, half a pint contains eight ounces of sugar, and so on.

(ii) Four ounces (110 grams) of sugar or a quarter of a pint (150 ml) of standard sugar syrup added to one gallon (4.5 litres) of wine will raise the specific gravity by about 0.010.

One question we have not so far considered is that of *when* a wine should be sweetened, that is immediately after the fermentation is over and the wine has cleared, or just before it is served? Careful analysis of the recipes submitted for this book reveals that the majority of winemakers sweeten their

TABLE 1
Amount of sugar in finished wines

Type of wine		Weight in ounces (grams) of granulated sugar required	
		Per 70 cl bottle	Per gallon/4.5 litres
Table	*Medium dry*	⅛ (3)	¾ (18)
	Medium sweet	½ (14)	3 (84)
	Sweet	1¼ (35)	7½ (210)
Aperitif	*Medium dry*	¼ (7)	1½ (42)
	Medium sweet	¾ (21)	4½ (126)
	Sweet	1½ (42)	9 (252)
Social	*Medium dry*	⅜ (11)	2¼ (66)
	Medium sweet	1 (28)	6 (168)
	Sweet	1¾ (49)	10½ (294)
Dessert	*Medium dry*	½ (14)	3 (84)
	Medium sweet	1¼ (35)	7½ (210)
	Sweet	2 (56)	12 (336)

This information is reproduced from the article "More About Sugar" by T. Edwin Belt, which appeared in the April 1983 issue of *Winemaker* magazine, by the kind permission of Argus Specialist Publications Limited.

wines soon after fermentation, when the wines are crystal clear and have been racked off the sediment. About half as many people prefer to sweeten their wine immediately before use, and one or two have achieved good results by sweetening the wine during storage, for example during the period of bulk maturing or when the wine is bottled and then laid down for some time. Each system has its own merits: the addition of sugar before storage may possibly give the components of the wine a greater chance to blend together and thus produce a more "coherent" drink, while adding the sugar immediately before use avoids all danger of refermentation in the bottle or demijohn.

Finally, a brief description of the uses of glycerol would not be out of place. Pure glycerol (also known as glycerine) is a sweet, dense liquid which is formed naturally during fermentation and contributes to the body of the wine. It follows that the addition of glycerol can add body, confer a smoother texture and slightly sweeten a wine. In addition glycerol is sometimes used to "mellow" an over-acidic or astringent wine. Most often, though, it is added to dessert-style wines to increase their body and give a smoother drink, and it is specified for this reason in many of the prizewinning dessert wine recipes in this book.

Maturation and storage

During storage, a series of slow chemical changes in a wine bring about the development of a good bouquet and flavour. A certain amount of oxygen is needed during the early stages of this maturation process; however, over-exposure to air will cause over-oxidation and produce a sherry-type flavour. Winemakers who have access to bulk storage facilities in wood casks can be fairly certain that their wine is receiving at least some oxygen since air can filter through pores in the wood. For most winemakers, however, who make single gallons (4.5 litres) of wine and store the wine in glass demijohns, it is the air introduced during racking which will play a significant part in encouraging the chemical changes necessary to produce a good wine. This is why several experts have suggested that red wines stored in glass demijohns after fermentation should be racked every three months for about one year. (See, for example, Mr R. N. Brooksbank's observations on storage in his recipe for Bilberry and Elderberry Dry Red Table Wine.) According to this theory, the wine can then be bottled or left undisturbed for a further period during which the bouquet will continue to develop and other changes such as the precipitation of tannin will continue.

That is the theory, but what of the practice? We can perhaps get some idea of the best way to mature home-made wine by analysing the way in which prizewinning wines are stored. An analysis of all the recipes submitted for this book which specifically describe the maturation procedure used by the winemaker concerned reveals the following facts.

(i) White table wines are stored in bulk in the demijohn after the end of fermentation for an average period of seven and a half months. During this time, they are racked no more than is necessary to remove the wine off the sediment. (Almost no white table wines are stored for more than twelve months in the demijohn.) These wines are then bottled, and generally either consumed almost immediately or stored for a further period of up to eighteen months; this extra storage is, however, very much the exception and usually only occurs when a wine has been bottled very soon after the end of fermentation. The question naturally arises as to whether home-made white wines are drunk so quickly simply through impatience and inexperience, and whether they would as a rule improve with keeping for, say, two years. The example of the better commercially produced white wines suggests that this may indeed often be so. However, we must keep in mind that these storage times may not be essential for success, since several of the prizewinning white table wines described in this book were bottled soon after the fermentation was over and exhibited while very young. This emphasizes the importance of experience and judgement in deciding when a wine is at its best.

(ii) Prizewinning white dessert wines are on average stored for eighteen months before use, a minimum of twelve months of this time being in the demijohn and the remaining time in the bottle. During the period of storage in the demijohn, the wines are racked no more than is necessary to remove the sediment. (Of course this does not mean that such a wine cannot be drunk before it has been stored for eighteen months;

the point is that these prizewinning wines have received the treatment described here.)

(iii) Red table wines give possibly the clearest picture of all. The average period of storage in demijohn after fermentation is over is twelve months; few wines are stored in bulk for less or more than this time. During this period, the wine may be racked more than is strictly necessary to remove the sediment, thereby aerating it, but this practice does not appear to be very widespread — possibly because its importance has not been recognized.

After this first twelve-month period, most home-made red wines are either bottled and drunk fairly soon, or bottled and left undisturbed for at least another six months — and often much longer. (In a few cases, however, the bottling is delayed and the wine is left undisturbed in the demijohn to mature further.)

Bearing in mind that some home winemakers store their wines for several years in bulk *and* in bottle, and that many prizewinning wines are several years old, it seems likely that most home-made red table wines would benefit from a longer period of bottle storage than they generally receive.

Finally, prizewinning red dessert wines also show a clear pattern: they are stored on average for two years, and at least twelve months of this time is spent in a demijohn. During the period of storage in bulk, the wine may be racked specially to aerate it.

No matter how long a wine is left to mature before it is bottled, two points should be kept in mind. First, storage containers should be kept topped up to avoid oxidation. Second, a wine often develops what is known as "bottle sickness" just after it has been bottled. This is a temporary dull lifelessness which seems to be caused by the introduction of air during bottling. So give your wine at least one month in the bottle, and preferably nearer three, to "recover" before you use it.

Blending

A significant number of winemakers prefer to blend their wines to achieve best results, rather than aim for a potential prizewinner from the word go. Of course this is good wine-making practice, for the skilful blending of wines with complementary faults can cancel the defects out and produce a good wine. However, the great majority of winemakers clearly prefer to rely on a recipe which uses a set of ingredients likely to produce a wine of quality that does not need to be blended later, and here they will find the recipes in this book of great value.

Shows and competitions

Suppose that you have produced a wine which you believe to be of competition standard. There is certainly no shortage of opportunities for you to enter your wine in a suitable show. To start with, there are shows run by local councils, horticultural societies, Women's Institutes, and so forth. Unfortunately, so I believe from those who have judged at such venues, the standard of entry in this type of competition is extremely variable. Next, there are shows held by local winemakers' circles or societies. These societies often encourage people to improve the standard of their home-made wine; certainly if you are at all interested in the hobby you would find it well worth joining one. (Your local reference library will probably have a list of local societies, among which you will almost certainly find a wine circle.)

There are also shows and festivals held by Regional Federations of Wine Circles. The North-West Federation of Amateur Winemaking Societies, for example, holds an annual show which attracts an entry of approximately two thousand bottles in thirty classes covering every conceivable type of wine. The standard is high, but this should not put you off "having a go". As one of my correspondents commented, "In an inter-club knockout competition I was rather deflated by a knowledgeable gentleman who commented: 'It's a bit thin, not much acid, no bouquet and lacking alcohol.' Waste of time putting it in, I thought, but in the event it won first prize! So to all winemakers I would say, put it in and have a go!" There's a lot of truth in this, and what makes the advice more valuable is that many shows have what is called a "judges at the bar" session, where the judge will be available to discuss your wine and suggest how it might be improved.

Finally, there is the National Show, the most prestigious amateur winemaking show in the country. It is organized by the National Association of Wine and Beermakers (Amateur) and each year attracts thousands of entries. To come first in a class at "The National" is indeed an achievement!

You may wonder who judges all these shows. Each Regional Federation of Wine Circles has its own list of qualified judges who can be called upon to judge at local wine circle shows as well as the regional or national events. There is also a National Guild of Wine and Beer Judges, an organization whose members have to pass a strict exam, and who should apply a standard judging procedure laid down in the Guild Handbook.

If you consider entering a competition, the first thing to do is obtain a copy of the show schedule from the show secretary. Next, decide which wines you will enter in which classes, bearing in mind the advice about defining your wine by taste and appearance rather than hydrometer readings! Do make sure you follow the rules about ingredients, bottle presentation and labelling, otherwise you will lose points unnecessarily. The judge may award maximum marks as follows: two for presentation; four for clarity and colour; four for bouquet; and twenty for flavour, balance and quality. To achieve these marks, the bottle and stopper need to be clean and bright, the wine must be perfectly clear with no trace of any deposit, the bouquet should be well developed and hint of the taste to come, and the taste should be well-balanced, pleasant, and correctly dry or sweet for the class. Clearly it helps in assessing how well your wine is likely to do on each of the criteria if you can identify the various faults and characteristics of wine before you enter a competition!

Finally, perhaps I should conclude this section with a quotation which can help us to keep things in perspective. This comes from another of my correspondents, who observes: "Making wine is a good hobby; drinking wine is a pleasurable pastime; winning a competition is a bonus!"

PART II

Recipes for Prizewinning Wines

A number of points which relate to all wine fermentations can be listed here for convenience.

(i) The length of pulp fermentation is generally accepted as being measured from the time when signs of fermentation such as foaming or fruit rising to the surface of the must first become visible. If a vigorous yeast preparation is added to the must, the delay between adding the yeast and fermentation actually beginning (a period when the yeast colony is building up in size and strength) should be reduced to a minimum.

(ii) The temperature at which the fermentation is conducted obviously controls to some extent the overall duration of the fermentation. It has been suggested that a slower fermentation can produce a better quality wine; however, below 15°C (60°F) the yeast may slow down or even stop. At the other end of the scale, temperatures in excess of 24°C (75°F) should generally be avoided. Consistency of temperature is most important in ensuring a smooth fermentation, and an electrical heating mat, demijohn belt, or thermostatic immersion heater is extremely useful in this respect.

(iii) When a recipe requires liquid to be strained off fruit pulp or other solid material, the straining should be done carefully, using both coarse and fine filter mesh if possible. This is the most practical way to exclude pulp sediment, which is often suspected of contributing off-flavours to a wine, from the demijohn. In addition, the pulp should not be pressed hard, for this will just purée the fruit and allow it to pass through the strainer. A better technique is to roll the pulp back and forth on the mesh and if necessary wash it with water.

(iv) An air-space over the wine in a fermentation jar fitted with an air-lock will not be harmful, for it will fill with inert carbon dioxide. However, when the wine is racked off the yeast sediment at the end of the fermentation, the air-space must be removed by topping up to the base of the demijohn neck, otherwise the wine may oxidize and turn dark. Incidentally, not all demijohns have a capacity of exactly one gallon (4.5 litres), but the slight variation in volume is of little significance and unlikely to affect the recipe. The important thing is not to find that you have added too much water to a fermentation bin or bucket, with the unhappy result that the volume of your strained must exceeds the size of your demijohn!

(v) Many wines foam vigorously when transferred to a demijohn until the yeast has used up all the oxygen and the slower anaerobic fermentation begins. It is therefore a useful precaution not to top up the must in a demijohn to its full volume until the first vigorous fermentation has died down. Of course if a recipe calls for later additions of sugar or grape concentrate, the demijohn will not be full at this stage anyway.

(vi) After fermentation, rack the wine off the yeast sediment as soon as possible to avoid the danger — however slight — of the yeast beginning to decay and so tainting the wine. One or two Campden tablets can be added per gallon (4.5 litres) as a precaution against oxidation and bacterial infection. Some winemakers prefer to use a stock solution of sodium metabisulphite rather than Campden tablets. This is made up by dissolving four ounces (110 grams) of sodium metabisulphite in two pints (1.15 litres) of water. One teaspoonful, or 5 ml, of this solution is equivalent to one Campden tablet.

(vii) The *teaspoonfuls* (tsp) in the recipes refer to a level standard teaspoonful (about 5 ml). *Tablespoonfuls* are indicated thus: tbsp.

(viii) Do ensure that all your equipment is thoroughly clean and sterile, by using sodium metabisulphite, Chempro SDP, Milton, or some other suitable sterilizing agent.

(ix) Almost all the recipes in this book were formulated in British (Imperial) Units. However, the conversion to Metric and American measures involves only very slight variations, so if you use either of these systems, you will still get good results. Some information on converting from one system to another is provided in the Appendix.

Apple Wine
(Dry White)

MR JOHN DILLEY OF SANDIACRE, NOTTINGHAMSHIRE

FIRST PRIZE, DRY WHITE WINE CLASS, ILKESTON FESTIVAL 1978

Imperial (Metric)
For 2 gallons (9 litres):
12 lb (5.4 kg) apples
2 lb (900 g) raisins
1 pint (550 ml) concentrated
    white grape juice
1 tsp dried elderflowers
2 lb (900 g) sugar
pectic enzyme
yeast nutrient
yeast (Sauternes)
water to 2 gallons (9 litres)

American

10 lb apples
1¾ lb raisins
1 pint concentrated white
    grape juice
1 tsp dried elderflowers
1¾ lb sugar
pectic enzyme
yeast nutrient
yeast (Sauternes)
water to 2 gallons

Liquidize the apples and transfer the pulp to a fermentation bin or bucket containing 10 pints (5.5 litres) of water in which 2 Campden tablets have been dissolved. Add the chopped raisins and sugar (dissolved in hot water and then allowed to cool), together with the dried elderflowers, pectic enzyme and nutrients. Cover and leave for twenty-four hours.

Add an active yeast starter and make the volume up to just under 2 gallons (9 litres). Cover and ferment for four days, stirring daily. Then strain through a fine mesh strainer into two 1-gallon (4.5-litre) demijohns and top up each to the gallon level with half the concentrate and water as necessary. Fit airlocks and leave to ferment to dryness; the final s.g. should be 1.000. Rack and top up as normal, adding a Campden tablet after the racking. Rack again when the wine is perfectly clear. Mature appropriately (about one year).

Apple Wine
(Dry White Table Wine)

MR M.E. HART OF THREE RIVERS WINE CIRCLE

FIRST PRIZE, WHITE DRY TABLE WINE CLASS,
ESSEX WINEMAKERS' FEDERATION SHOW 1985

Imperial (Metric)

4½ lb (2 kg) mixed cooking and eating apples
1½ lb (700 g) ornamental crab apples
1¾ pints (1 litre) white grape juice (natural strength)
2 lb (900 g) sugar
pectic enzyme
1 Vitamin B tablet
yeast and nutrient
water to 1 gallon (4.5 litres)

American

4 lb mixed cooking and eating apples
1½ lb ornamental crab apples
1¾ pints white grape juice (natural strength)
1¾ lb sugar
pectic enzyme
1 Vitamin B tablet
yeast and nutrient
water to 1 gallon

Wash the fruit, drain it and then freeze it hard. This will break down the tissue. While the apples are still whole and frozen, place them in a fermentation bucket with 2 Campden tablets and add 6 pints (3.5 litres) of boiling water. When the fruit and water has cooled sufficiently to handle it, break up the apples using sterilized rubber gloves or carefully washed bare hands. Keep the fruit immersed while doing so to avoid oxidation. Add 2 tsp pectic enzyme, then cover and leave for twenty-four hours in a warm place.

Twenty-four hours later, add the grape juice, Vitamin B tablet and an active yeast starter and nutrient. Cover and allow to ferment for seven days, stirring daily to break up the fruit cap. Then strain into a fresh bucket, stir in the sugar and, when the frothing subsides, pour into a demijohn. Fit an air-lock and leave the wine to ferment out. Rack as required, adding a Campden tablet each time and keeping the jar well topped up with boiled water.

[*Note:* I have used exactly this procedure with crab apples and found that it works well. However, the finished wine had a hint of almond flavour, presumably due to the pips being ruptured during the freezing. Whether or not this develops may depend on how hard the apples are frozen — Ed.]

Apple Wine
(Dry White Table Wine)

MR BRIAN KEER OF NEWQUAY, CORNWALL

FIRST PRIZE, THREE WINES FOR A DINNER CLASS,
SOUTH-WESTERN COUNTIES WINE AND BEERMAKERS'
FEDERATION FESTIVAL 1981

Imperial (Metric)
7 lb (3.2 kg) apples
½ pint (300 ml) concentrated
    white grape juice

American
6 lb apples
½ pint concentrated white
    grape juice

2 lb (900 g) sugar
1 tsp tartaric acid
1 tsp Pectolase
2 tsp yeast nutrient
yeast (Unican all-purpose)
water to 1 gallon (4.5 litres)

1¾ lb sugar
1 tsp tartaric acid
1 tsp Pectolase
2 tsp yeast nutrient
yeast (Unican all-purpose)
water to 1 gallon

Make a yeast starter before preparing the wine.

The juice can be extracted from the apples with a Saftborn or Mehu-Maija steam juicer. This will yield about 3 pints (1.7 litres) of sterile juice. [An alternative would be to crush and press the apples — Ed.] Let the juice cool and then add the rest of the ingredients with the exception of the yeast. Dissolve 1 Campden tablet in the must, transfer to a demijohn and top up with cool boiled water to the bottom of the shoulder of the jar. Plug the neck and leave to stand overnight.

Next day, add the yeast and fit an air-lock. When the initial vigorous fermentation has subsided, top up to the base of the neck with cool, boiled water. Ferment to completion.

Rack off the sediment and add a Campden tablet. Top up with a bland white wine of light colour and low alcohol content. Rack again when the wine is two months old, and add another Campden tablet. Four months later the wine will be ready for bottling, but this time do not add another Campden tablet.

This wine is best drunk while still fairly young — say a year to eighteen months.

[The two accompanying prize wines were Mr Keer's Dried Elderberry Table Wine and his Bilberry, Elderberry and Black-berry Dessert Wine, both of which are included in this book — Ed.]

Apple "Champagne"

MR DON SAYERS OF PEASMARSH, EAST SUSSEX

FIRST PRIZE, MAIDSTONE WINEMAKERS' SHOW

Mr Sayers has kindly provided these detailed instructions for his sparkling apple wine.

"I would not advise beginners to attempt making this wine, as very precise control of the process is necessary, otherwise serious accidents can occur. The standard champagne bottle will withstand a pressure of approximately 90 pounds per square inch. If this is exceeded the bottle can burst like a bomb. So before you start, examine the bottles for deep scratches or flaws and discard any you are in doubt about. Finally, check the weight of the bottle. Those that don't bump 2 lb (900 g) on the scale are not strong enough.

"Select the type of wine most suitable. I prefer an apple wine made from the juice of 80% Bramleys and the rest mixed apples. Store the fruit in trays until about the end of November, when the acid content has fallen and the sugar content has risen. The juice has to be extracted either by using a juice extractor or by crushing and pressing. It must then be suitably protected against oxidation by the addition of one 50 mg Vitamin C tablet and one Campden tablet per gallon (4.5 litres).

"The next important aspect is not to let the sugar in the must exceed 2 lb (900 g) per gallon (4.5 litres) otherwise you won't get the secondary fermentation in the bottle. So measure the initial s.g. of the juice using a hydrometer: in an average year the initial sugar content of the juice from apples on my trees is 1¼ lb (570 g) per gallon (4.5 litres). This means only 12 oz (340 g) of extra sugar is needed. The aim is to adjust the initial s.g. of the must to 1.080. Add the usual nutrients and a quick-fermenting yeast such as Vinquick from Southern

Vineyards. Aim for a rapid fermentation down to s.g. 0.990 in ten to fourteen days; this will require a fermentation temperature of 24°C (75°F)±1°. If the fermentation does not produce a dry wine of s.g. 0.990, don't use it for making sparkling wine.

"Rack the wine and transfer it to a cool place to accelerate its clearing; do not, however, add any Campden tablets. You should aim to have the wine clear and bright in a few weeks.

"While waiting for the wine to clear, prepare the bottles by marking the filling level on the neck precisely three inches (seven centimetres) from the top. This distance is most important as it governs the final pressure in the bottle in conjunction with the rest of the procedure. Next, make up a standard sugar solution, i.e. 1 lb (450 g) of sugar dissolved in half a pint (285 ml) of boiling water, and prepare your plastic champagne stoppers and wire ties. Finally, the day before you are going to bottle your wine, prepare a yeast starter using a good Champagne yeast.

"Transfer the clear wine to a sterilized plastic bucket and add the active yeast and 3 fl oz (84 ml) of the standard sugar syrup. Measure this precisely, using a photographic measuring cylinder if possible — it's that critical. Mix well and then fill the bottles to the mark on the neck. Insert and wire down the stoppers. The wine can now be left to mature for about six months in an upright position.

"This procedure, if carried out correctly, will give an internal pressure of about 45 psi — well within the safety margin of secondhand bottles, and low enough to prevent 'gushing' when the bottles are opened. The small amount of yeast sediment from the secondary fermentation is very small and firm on the bottom. If the wine is required for exhibition, then the wine bottles must be disgorged, a procedure well described in other books on the subject." [See, for example, *Home Winemaking Techniques and Recipes* — Ed.]

Apple and Elderflower Wine
(Dry White Table Wine)

MR H. APPLEBY OF SALE, CHESHIRE

THIRD PRIZE, DRY WHITE OR GOLD TABLE WINE CLASS,
NORTH-WEST FEDERATION SHOW 1983

Imperial (Metric)

1¾ pints (1 litre) pure apple juice

8 oz (250 g) concentrated white grape juice

1½ lb (700 g) sugar

¼ oz (10 g) dried elderflowers

1 tsp tartaric acid

1 tsp Pectolase

1 tsp yeast nutrient

yeast

water to 1 gallon (4.5 litres)

American

1¾ pints pure apple juice

8 oz concentrated white grape juice

1¼ lb sugar

¼ oz dried elderflowers

1 tsp tartaric acid

1 tsp Pectolase

1 tsp yeast nutrient

yeast

water to 1 gallon

Put all the ingredients except the elderflowers into a demijohn and make up to 7 pints (4 litres) with cool, boiled water. Ferment under air-lock for seven days, then add the elderflowers and top up to the gallon (4.5 litres). Refit air-lock and ferment out to dryness (specific gravity of 0.990–0.995).

Add 1 Campden tablet, rack off the sediment and leave the wine in a cool place to clear. The wine may be fined or filtered as required. Bottle and leave for three to six months.

This wine is useful as a regular tipple for everyday drinking, and Mr Appleby makes it in 5-gallon (22.5-litre) batches, adding a carton of pineapple juice to the five of apple.

Apple and Gooseberry Table Wine
(Dry)

THIRD PRIZE, DRY WHITE FRUIT WINE CLASS,
LOCAL WINE CIRCLE COMPETITION 1986

Imperial (Metric)	**American**
3 lb (1.35 kg) canned or bottled gooseberries	2½ lb canned or bottled gooseberries
1¾ pints (1 litre) pure apple juice	1¾ pints pure apple juice
⅓ pint (200 ml) concentrated white grape juice	¼ pint concentrated white grape juice
1 lb 10 oz (750 g) sugar	1½ lb sugar
2 tsp tartaric acid	2 tsp tartaric acid
pectic enzyme	pectic enzyme
general-purpose yeast and nutrient	general-purpose yeast and nutrient
water to 1 gallon (4.5 litres)	water to 1 gallon

Prepare a yeast starter the day before making the wine.

Dissolve the sugar in about 2 pints (1.2 litres) of boiling water and pour the solution over the gooseberries, apple juice, acid and grape concentrate in a fermentation bucket. Make up the volume to 1 gallon (4.5 litres) with cool, boiled water then add the yeast, enzyme and nutrients. Cover and leave to ferment on the pulp for four days, ensuring the temperature is correct (18–21°C, 65–70°F). Mash the fruit with a spoon each day.

Then strain off the liquid into a demijohn, top up to the gallon (4.5 litres) if necessary, fit an air-lock and leave to ferment to dryness. Allow the yeast to form a firm sediment before racking the wine into a clean demijohn. Add 1 Campden tablet dissolved in a little water, and when the wine is perfectly clear, rack again. The wine can of course be fined with Bentonite or Isinglass if necessary. Bottle at once; the wine needs only a few months to mature and can be enjoyed before it is a year old.

Apricot Wine
(Dry or Dessert)

MR E.K. MITCHELL OF ROMILEY WINEMAKERS

THIRD PRIZE, WHITE OR GOLDEN DESSERT WINE CLASS,
NORTH-WEST FEDERATION SHOW 1985

Imperial (Metric)
4 lb (1.8 kg) fresh apricots
3 lb (1.35 kg) bananas
8 oz (225 g) muscatel raisins
sugar (see method)
1½ tsp tartaric acid
¼ tsp tannin
1 Vitamin B¹ tablet
high-alcohol-tolerance yeast
  and nutrient
water to 1 gallon (4.5 litres)

American
3½ lb fresh apricots
2½ lb bananas
8 oz muscatel raisins
sugar (see method)
1½ tsp tartaric acid
¼ tsp tannin
1 Vitamin B¹ tablet
high-alcohol-tolerance yeast
  and nutrient
water to 1 gallon

Boil the bananas in water for about ten minutes, then strain off the "juice" and place it in a fermentation bin or bucket. Place the raisins in boiling water and leave them to soak for three hours, before pouring off the water and transferring the raisins to the bucket. They should then be crushed, using a spoon or your hands. Liquidize the apricots and add the pulp to the bucket together with enough boiling water and sugar to bring the volume up to 7 pints (4.0 litres) and the specific gravity to 1.070.

Introduce the yeast starter and ferment on the pulp for four days, keeping well covered and stirring twice daily. Strain off and discard the pulp, and transfer the wine to a demijohn under air-lock. "Feed" the wine with sugar in 4 oz (110 g) lots until the wine reaches an alcohol level of 14–16%. [A total of roughly 3 lb/1.35 kg of sugar — Ed.] This should enable the yeast to produce a dry wine of specific gravity around 0.990. By then sweetening the wine to a specific gravity of 1.036–1.038, you will have a wine suitable for the dessert class in a show.

[The wine may be matured as appropriate for its use; some guidelines are provided in the section on maturation earlier in the book. — Ed.]

Apricot Wine
(Medium)

MR G. ROTHERHAM OF SOUTHPORT WINE CIRCLE

FIRST PRIZE, AINSDALE OPEN SHOW 1985

Imperial (Metric)
2 lb (900 g) dried apricots
1 lb (450 g) sultanas
1 banana
juice of 2 lemons
2 lb (900 g) sugar
1 tsp Pectolase
yeast and nutrient
water to 1 gallon (4.5 litres)

American
1¾ lb dired apricots
1 lb sultanas
1 banana
juice of 2 lemons
1¾ lb sugar
1 tsp Pectolase
yeast and nutrient
water to 1 gallon

Mince the apricots and sultanas and place them in a fermentation bucket with the sugar. Simmer the peeled, chopped banana for ten minutes and add the "juice" only to the bucket. Add a cup of black tea brewed in the normal way (preferably Darjeeling), and then make up to the gallon (4.5 litres) with boiling water. Cover and leave to cool overnight.

Next day, add the lemon juice, Pectolase, nutrient and an active yeast made up as a starter. Leave to ferment for nine to ten days, keeping well covered and stirring twice daily. Then strain into a demijohn, fit an air-lock and leave until fermentation has finished.

Rack off and top up as normal. The wine is best left for eighteen months to mature; it may be sweetened to taste.

Apricot Dessert Wine

MR BRIAN KEER OF NEWQUAY, CORNWALL

FIRST PRIZE, WHITE OR GOLDEN DESSERT WINE CLASS,
CORNISH WINE AND BEER CIRCLES ASSOCIATION SHOW 1982

Imperial (Metric)

*2 lb (900 g) dried apricots
(whole pieces, good
quality)*

*8 oz (225 g) peeled ripe
bananas*

*1 can (1 kg) concentrated
white grape juice (CWE
Original Sweet)*

sugar (see method)

½ tsp tartaric acid

4 drops liquid tannin solution

1 tsp Pectolase

*2 tsp Tronozymol yeast
nutrient*

1 Vitamin B¹ tablets

*wine yeast (Gervin Number
3)*

water to 1 gallon (4.5 litres)

American

*1¾ lb dried apricots (whole
pieces, good quality)*

8 oz peeled ripe bananas

*1 pint concentrated white
grape juice (CWE
Original Sweet)*

sugar (see method)

½ tsp tartaric acid

4 drops liquid tannin solution

1 tsp Pectolase

*2 tsp Tronozymol yeast
nutrient*

1 Vitamin B¹ tablet

*wine yeast (Gervin Number
3)*

water to 1 gallon

Simmer the apricots in 3 pints (1.7 litres) of water for ten minutes and then leave them to stand for thirty minutes. Simmer the peeled bananas in 2 pints (1.2 litres) of water for twenty minutes. Strain off the fruit pulp and place the liquid from both the bananas and apricots in a bucket. Allow to cool, then add the remainder of the ingredients (except the yeast) and 1 Campden tablet. A pinch of Epsom salts can also be added if available. Cover the bucket.

Next day, reconstitute the yeast in lukewarm water for five minutes, add it to the must, and pour the must into a demi-john. Fit an air-lock and leave it to ferment.

When the specific gravity falls to 1.005, dissolve 4 oz (110 g) of sugar in the wine and mix it in very thoroughly. Repeat the process each time the s.g. falls to 1.005. About 1½ lb (700 g) of sugar can be added this way.

When the fermentation is finally complete, rack the wine off the sediment and add 1 Campden tablet and sorbate to stabilize the wine. Top up with another dessert wine if possible; if not, any white wine, but don't use water since that would dilute the wine too much.

Rack again when the wine is two months old. Sweeten to taste and add another Campden tablet. After a further six months carry out one more racking and add a final Campden tablet. Bottle the wine when it is one year old; it will reach a peak between one year and eighteen months.

Apricot and Elderberry Rosé

MR ROY SMALES OF NOTTINGHAM

FIRST PRIZE, THE NATIONAL SHOW 1979

Imperial (Metric)
For two gallons (9 litres):
29 oz (800 g) canned apricots

American

1½ lb canned apricots

1 lb (450 g) sultanas	1 lb sultanas
4 oz (110 g) elderberries	4 oz elderberries
4 oz can (110 g) Birds Eye Florida Orange Juice (frozen)★	4 oz Birds Eye Florida Orange Juice (frozen)★
4 lb (1.8 kg) sugar	3½ lb sugar
3 tsp tartaric acid	3 tsp tartaric acid
2 tsp pectic enzyme	2 tsp pectic enzyme
¼ tsp tannin	¼ tsp tannin
3 tsp yeast nutrient	3 tsp yeast nutrient
yeast (Hock or all-purpose)	yeast (Hock or all-purpose)
water to 2 gallons (9 litres)	water to 2 gallons

★The orange juice can be found in the freezer compartments of most supermarkets.

For this method you will need a plastic bucket (with a lid) which will hold more than 2 gallons (9 litres).

Bring the sultanas to the boil in 2 pints (1.2 litres) of water; then pour away the water and chop up the sultanas. Bring the elderberries to the boil in 2 pints (1.2 litres) of water, but this time discard the fruit; only the liquid is used. Mix this with the chopped sultanas in the bucket and add another 10 pints (5.5 litres) of boiled water. Add 3 lb (1.35 kg) of sugar while the liquid is hot and stir until dissolved.

When the must has cooled to fermentation temperature, add all the other ingredients and ferment for five days. Keep the bucket covered.

Strain the liquid out of the bucket and divide it equally between 2 demijohns. Add ½ lb (225 g) of sugar dissolved in cool, boiled water to each demijohn and mix well. Top up each demijohn to 1 gallon (4.5 litres) with cool, boiled water, fit air-locks, and leave to finish fermenting — about four weeks.

Siphon the wine carefully into fresh demijohns, leaving behind the sediment. Add a wine-fining agent.

When clear, the wine can be bottled. This wine will be ready for drinking after only six months. As a rosé wine is usually medium sweet, 3 tsp sugar can be dissolved in each bottle just before drinking.

Barley Wine
(A Social Wine)

MR PETER WITHERDEN OF POOLE, DORSET

LOCAL CIRCLE PRIZEWINNING WINE

Imperial (Metric)
1 lb (450 g) barley
1½ lb (700 g) raisins
1 lb (450 g) overripe bananas
2¼ lb (1 kg) sugar
3 tsp tartaric acid
2 tsp yeast nutrient
1 Vitamin B¹ tablet
pectic enzyme
yeast
water to 1 gallon (4.5 litres)

American
1 lb barley
1¼ lb raisins
1 lb overripe bananas
1¾ lb sugar
3 tsp tartaric acid
2 tsp yeast nutrient
1 Vitamin B¹ tablet
pectic enzyme
yeast
water to 1 gallon

Peel and chop the bananas and boil the slices (without the skins) in 2 pints (1.2 litres) of water for thirty minutes. Strain the liquid into a sterilized container. Wash the barley and raisins thoroughly. Grind the barley in a coffee mill or put it through a mincer; chop or mince the raisins. Add both these ingredients to the banana "juice", together with the sugar and acid. Stir well to dissolve, then pour 4 pints (2.3 litres) of boiling water over the mixture and cover. When must is at fermentation temperature (about 24°C/75°F) add the pectic enzyme, nutrient and Vitamin B¹ tablet. Prepare a starter bottle for the yeast, and leave it with the must in a warm place until the following day.

Next day, ensure the must is at 24°C (75°F) and pour in the yeast. Stir and cover. Leave the must in the bucket for four days, stirring daily. After this period, strain through a fine muslin or nylon mesh strainer into a sterile demijohn and fit an air-lock. Top up to neck of jar with water after one week and ferment to dryness.

Carry out the usual racking, sulphiting, storage and bottling. Add sugar syrup to sweeten to taste before drinking or showing; social wine usually has a final specific gravity between 1.005 and 1.010.

Note: if the wine fails to clear after six to nine months, there might be a haze in the wine due to the starch content of the barley. The use of amylase enzyme will clear this.

"Beaujolais"

DOWNLEY WINE AND BEER CIRCLE
WINNER, CHILTERN AND MID-THAMES FESTIVAL

Imperial (Metric)	**American**
1½ lb (700 g) blackberries	1¼ lb blackberries
4 oz (110 g) elderberries	4 oz elderberries
4 oz (110 g) raspberries	4 oz raspberries
2 oz (60 g) blackcurrants	2 oz blackcurrants
½ pint (300 ml) concentrated red grape juice	½ pint concentrated red grape juice
2¼ lb (1 kg) sugar	1¾ lb sugar
2 tsp citric acid	2 tsp citric acid
2 tsp tartaric acid	2 tsp tartaric acid
1 tsp Pectolase	1 tsp Pectolase
yeast (Burgundy) and nutrient	yeast (Burgundy) and nutrient
water to 1 gallon (4.5 litres)	water to 1 gallon

Wash the fruit and place it in a bucket with 6 pints (3.5 litres)

of cold water containing 1 dissolved Campden tablet. Stir, cover and leave for twenty-four hours. Then add half of the sugar, being careful to ensure it is completely dissolved, the grape juice and all the other ingredients. Make the volume up to just under 1 gallon (4.5 litres) and leave to ferment for four or five days, keeping well covered and stirring twice daily.

Strain into a demijohn, adding the rest of the sugar dissolved in enough water to bring the volume up to the gallon (4.5 litres). Fit an air-lock and ferment to dryness. Rack and mature as normal.

Bilberry Wine
(Dry Red Wine)

SECOND PRIZE, DRY RED FRUIT WINE CLASS,
LOCAL CIRCLE COMPETITION 1986

Imperial (Metric)
*3 lb (1.35 kg) bottled
  bilberries
  or 3 lb (1.35 kg) fresh
  bilberries
  or 12 oz (350 g) dried
  bilberries
1/3 pint (200 ml) concentrated
  red grape juice
1 lb 14 oz (840 g) sugar
1 tsp tartaric acid
1/4 tsp grape tannin
pectic enzyme
yeast and nutrient
water to 1 gallon (4.5 litres)*

American
*2 1/2 lb bottled bilberries

  or 2 1/2 lb fresh bilberries

  or 10 oz dried bilberries

1/3 pint concentrated red grape
  juice
1 1/2 lb sugar
1 tsp tartaric acid
1/4 tsp grape tannin
pectic enzyme
yeast and nutrient
water to 1 gallon*

Wash both fresh and dried berries in water before using them to remove any sticks, leaves and so forth. If the fresh berries are small and sour, and with dried berries in any case, heat the berries in about 5 pints (2.8 litres) of water to boiling point and add the sugar. Stir to dissolve and leave to cool. Otherwise pour 5 pints (2.8 litres) of boiling water in which the sugar has been dissolved over the fruit in a fermentation bin and leave to cool. *Note:* if you are using bottled fruit, try to adjust the quantity of sugar added so that the initial specific gravity is around 1.085.

When the fruit and liquid has cooled to the correct fermentation temperature, mash the fruit gently, then add the remaining ingredients and an active yeast starter. Make the volume up to 1 gallon (4.5 litres), cover and allow to ferment on the pulp for three days, stirring three times daily.

Strain into a demijohn through a fine nylon or muslin strainer, top up if necessary, fit an air-lock and ferment to completion. Rack when the wine has cleared somewhat, and again when it is completely clear, adding 1 Campden tablet each time. Store for at least six months before sampling. A dessertspoon each of sugar and glycerine in a gallon will add a little extra smoothness. The prize wine was produced using fresh berries and was matured for twelve months.

Bilberry and Elderberry Wine
(Dry Red Table Wine)

MR R.N. BROOKSBANK OF BEESTON, NOTTINGHAM

FIRST PRIZE, THREE BOTTLES FOR A DINNER CLASS,
THE NATIONAL SHOW 1985

Imperial (Metric)
For 5 gallons (22.5 litres):
6 lb (2.7 kg) bottled bilberries
4 lb (1.8 kg) elderberries

American

5 lb bottled bilberries
3½ lb elderberries

2 cans (2 kg) concentrated red grape juice★	2 pints concentrated red grape juice★
1 can (1 kg) concentrated white grape juice★	1 pint concentrated white grape juice★
5¼ pints (3 litres) apple juice	5¼ pints apple juice
4½ lb (2 kg) sugar	3¾ lb sugar
1 oz (30 g) grape tannin powder	¾ oz grape tannin powder
8 tsp pectic enzyme	8 tsp pectic enzyme
8 tsp (40 ml) lactic acid	8 tsp lactic acid
8 tsp (40 ml) acetic acid (30%)	8 tsp acetic acid (30%)
yeast (Burgundy)	yeast (Burgundy)
water to 5 gallons (22.5 litres)	water to 5 gallons

★Best quality concentrate: try to find the type without added citric acid.

Make a starter bottle with claret or burgundy yeast. When the yeast is fermenting well, put it in a clean demijohn with the tin of white concentrate and add water to the shoulder of the jar. Leave until fermentation begins. When this happens, pour 2 gallons (9 litres) of boiling water on the elderberries and stir for ten minutes. Sterilize a large fermentation vessel and put the other ingredients into it with 1 gallon (4.5 litres) of water; then add the hot water with the elderberries. When the temperature is about 20°C (70°F), pour in the gallon (4.5 litres) of fermenting grape juice. Stir it all thoroughly and leave to ferment for three days, pushing down the pulp twice a day.

Next, strain off the pulp and make the wine up to 5 gallons (22.5 litres) with cold tap water. The addition of 3 oz (90 g) of oak sawdust or small chips at this stage will help the wine to mature more quickly and give a commercial type flavour; however, the oak must be sound, dry and fresh. Its effect is marked, and has been found to improve several red wines.

Stir the wine once a day for a week, then let it ferment out to dryness (specific gravity about 0.992). When all the bubbling has stopped, leave it for another week to settle, then siphon it off and add 5 Campden tablets, stirring thoroughly.

The wine may be matured in either of two ways:

(i) Leave it to clear in an ex-wine 5-gallon (22.5-litre) container for a month, then siphon it into a cask. Top up the cask every week for about a year, then siphon it off and add 5 Campden tablets. (If the wine needs clearing, use Bentonite or Isinglass.) Bottle the wine in airtight pop bottles and store them upright. If a surface yeast forms, the cap or stopper is leaking air.

(ii) If no cask is available, pour the wine into demijohns and rack off any deposit every month for six months, then every two months for the next six months. After this period, proceed as in (i) for bottling.

The wine may well taste disappointing at bottling time, but after six months it will be much better. Some time after a year in bottle, there can be a complete transformation of the wine, like a butterfly emerging from a chrysalis. The individual ingredients seem to merge together to form a completely different wine, and "elderberries" and "bilberries" disappear. The prize wine was five years old and looks good for at least another five, with a claret type of bouquet and softening flavour.

Bilberry, Elderberry and Blackberry Wine

(Dessert Wine)

MR BRIAN KEER OF NEWQUAY, CORNWALL

FIRST-PRIZE, THREE WINES FOR A DINNER CLASS.
SOUTH-WESTERN COUNTIES WINE AND BEERMAKERS'
FEDERATION FESTIVAL 1981

Imperial (Metric)
2 lb (900 g) bilberries bottled
    in syrup
    or 2 lb (900 g) fresh
    bilberries
1 lb (450 g) elderberries
    (frozen)
1 lb (450 g) blackberries
    (frozen)
1 lb (450 g) seedless raisins
36 fl oz (1 litre) concentrated
    red grape juice
sugar (see method)
1 tsp tartaric acid
1 tsp malic acid
1 tsp Pectolase
2 tsp Tronozymol yeast
    nutrient
1 Vitamin B1 tablet
Rohament P
wine yeast (preferably Gervin
    Number 3)
water to 1 gallon (4.5 litres)

American
1¾ lb bilberries bottled in
    syrup
    or 1¾ lb fresh bilberries
1 lb elderberries (frozen)
1 lb blackberries (frozen)
1 lb seedless raisins
2 pints concentrated red grape
    juice
sugar (see method)
1 tsp tartaric acid
1 tsp malic acid
1 tsp Pectolase
2 tsp Tronozymol yeast
    nutrient
1 Vitamin B1 tablet
Rohament P
wine yeast (preferably Gervin
    Number 3)
water to 1 gallon

Prepare a yeast starter before making the wine.

Thaw out the elderberries and blackberries, then place them in a fermentation bin or bucket together with the bilberries, chopped raisins and 5 pints (2.8 litres) of cold water. Dissolve 1 crushed Campden tablet in the must and add the pectic enzyme and one capful of Rohament P. Stir well.

Next day introduce the rest of the ingredients except the grape concentrate and sugar. Mix well. (A pinch of Epsom salts can also be added at this stage if available.) Leave to ferment on the pulp for two days, stirring twice daily but otherwise keeping covered.

Next, strain into a demijohn and add 1 pint (600 ml) of the grape juice concentrate; mix well. Do not top up yet, but fit an air-lock and ferment until the specific gravity falls to 1.005. Then add a further 8 fl oz (230 ml) of concentrate. Repeat the process when the specific gravity again falls to 1.005, but use only 4 fl oz (120 ml) of concentrate. (The last 4 fl oz is used to sweeten the wine when fermentation is complete.)

Keep checking the specific gravity, and each time it falls to 1.005 stir in 4 oz (110 g) of sugar. Ensure each addition is dissolved and mixed in well. Repeat until the fermentation is complete.

Rack the wine off the sediment into a clean container and stabilize with potassium sorbate and a Campden tablet in the normal way. Top up with the remaining grape concentrate and another red dessert wine if possible. If one is not available, then an ordinary red wine will do, but don't use water as this will dilute the wine too much.

Rack at two months and sweeten to taste. Then rack at six monthly intervals if necessary. Don't add any sulphite at these rackings, because the oxygen absorbed will help to mature the wine. Keep for at least two years.

[The two accompanying prize wines were Mr Keer's Dry Apple Table Wine and his Dried Elderberry Table Wine, both of which are included in this book — Ed.]

Blackberry Wine
(Dry)

MR DON SAYERS OF PEASMARSH, EAST SUSSEX

Imperial (Metric)
4 lb (1.8 kg) blackberries
8 oz (225 g) raisins
1¾ lb (800 g) white sugar
4 oz (110 g) dark brown
  sugar
1 Vitamin B¹ tablet
1 tsp Pectolase
1 tsp yeast nutrient★
yeast (general-purpose)
water to 1 gallon (4.5 litres)

American
3½ lb blackberries
8 oz raisins
1½ lb white sugar
4 oz dark brown sugar

1 Vitamin B¹ tablet
1 tsp Pectolase
1 tsp yeast nutrient★
yeast (general-purpose)
water to 1 gallon

★Mr Sayers used 1 tsp of Grey Owl nutrient and ½ tsp of Grey Owl yeast energizer.

Put the blackberries and roughly chopped raisins into a fermentation bin or bucket and pour on 6 pints (3.5 litres) of boiling water. Stir in 8 oz (225 g) of white sugar and allow to cool. At fermentation temperature, add the pectic enzyme and yeast. Cover with a cloth and ferment on the pulp for three days.

Strain the liquid into a clean demijohn and add the rest of the sugar dissolved in enough water to bring the volume up to 1 gallon (4.5 litres). The yeast nutrients and Vitamin B¹ tablet should also be added at this stage. (A 20 mg Vitamin C tablet can also be dissolved in the wine as a precaution against oxidation.) Fit an air-lock and ferment to dryness. Rack into a clean jar and add 2 Campden tablets. Keep for one year in a cool place.

Blackberry Social Wine

MR PETER WITHERDEN OF POOLE, DORSET

THIRD PRIZE, DRY RED TABLE WINE CLASS,
THE NATIONAL SHOW 1976

Imperial (Metric)	**American**
3½ lb (1.6 kg) blackberries	3 lb blackberries
1 lb (450 g) overripe bananas	1 lb overripe bananas
2½ lb (1.15 kg) sugar	2 lb sugar
½ tsp acid	½ tsp acid
1 Vitamin B¹ tablet	1 Vitamin B¹ tablet
pectic enzyme	pectic enzyme
yeast nutrient	yeast nutrient
yeast (Port or general-purpose)	yeast (Port or general-purpose)
water to 1 gallon (4.5 litres)	water to 1 gallon

Sterilize and soften the blackberries by bringing them to the boil in 3 pints (1.7 litres) of water. Peel and chop the bananas and boil them in a nylon bag in 1 pint (550 ml) of water for thirty minutes. Remove the bananas from the water and discard. Pour the water together with the blackberries and their liquid on to 2 lb (900 g) of sugar in a sterilized bucket. Stir, cover and allow to cool to about 25°C (75°F). Add 1 tsp pectic enzyme. Make up a yeast starter bottle.

Next day, make the must up to 7 pints (4 litres) with tap water and add the nutrients. If possible, adjust the acid as necessary to 4 p.p.t., and add enough of the remaining sugar to bring the specific gravity up to 1.100. Add the active yeast from the starter bottle, stir and cover. Ferment at 25°C (75°F), stirring twice daily for three days.

On the fifth day, strain the must through a nylon sieve and funnel the liquid into a sterile demijohn. Top up as necessary, fit an air-lock and ferment to dryness — about three weeks. The final specific gravity will be 1.000 or less.

Rack into a clean jar, top up with water and refit air-lock. Store at a temperature of 18°C (65°F) if possible. Rack every two or three months, adding a Campden tablet at the second and fourth rackings. Top up with water and refit air-lock each time.

Bottle at one year and leave to mature for a further six months at a temperature of about 13°C (55°F). Before drinking or showing, add sugar syrup to sweeten to taste. The final specific gravity of a social wine is usually between 1.005 and 1.010.

Note: To increase the vinosity, the recipe can be varied by reducing the blackberries to 2½ lb (1.15 kg) and adding ½ pint (300 ml) of grape concentrate.

Blackberry Wine
(Sweet)

MRS B. WATSON OF NEWLANDS WINE CIRCLE

GOLD MEDAL WINNER, CARLISLE AREA COMPETITION 1982

Imperial (Metric)
3½ lb (1.6 kg) blackberries
8 oz (225 g) raisins
3 lb (1.35 kg) sugar
pectic enzyme
yeast and nutrient
water to 1 gallon (4.5 litres)

American
3 lb blackberries
8 oz raisins
2½ lb sugar
pectic enzyme
yeast and nutrient
water to 1 gallon

Wash the fruit and place it in a pan containing 4 pints (2.3 litres) of water. Bring to the boil and boil gently for one minute. Remove from heat and pour both fruit and liquid into a fermentation vessel with the chopped raisins. Allow to cool, then add the pectic enzyme, yeast and nutrient. Cover and leave for four days, stirring twice daily.

Then strain carefully through nylon mesh or muslin onto the sugar. Stir thoroughly until the sugar has dissolved and transfer to a demijohn. Top up to the shoulder of the jar, fit an air-lock and leave to ferment. When the first vigorous fermentation has died away, top up to the neck and leave to ferment in the normal way. Rack when clear. This wine is a good one to blend with elderberry.

Blackberry Wine
(Sweet)

FIRST PRIZE, SWEET RED CLASS, LOCAL WINE CIRCLE SHOW 1985

Imperial (Metric)
6 lb (2.7 kg) blackberries
8 oz (225 g) currants
½ pint (300 ml) concentrated red grape juice
12 oz (350 g) golden syrup
8 oz (225 g) liquid malt extract
1¼ lb (550 g) sugar
2 tsp tartaric acid
pectic enzyme
yeast and nutrient
water to 1 gallon (4.5 litres)

American
5 lb blackberries
8 oz currants
½ pint concentrated red grape juice
10 oz golden syrup
8 oz liquid malt extract
1 lb sugar
2 tsp tartaric acid
pectic enzyme
yeast and nutrient
water to 1 gallon

Wash the currants in hot water to remove the oil they are packed in, then chop them roughly and transfer to a pan containing 5 pints (2.8 litres) of water. Bring to the boil and simmer gently for about ten minutes, then add the blackberries, golden syrup, sugar and acid. Simmer gently for five minutes, stirring the mixture, then add the malt extract and remove from the heat. Allow to cool, then transfer the whole mass to a fermentation bin and make the volume up to the gallon (4.5 litres). Introduce the pectic enzyme and a yeast starter, stir, cover and leave to ferment for four days, keeping well covered and stirring daily.

At the end of this time, strain into a demijohn and add the concentrate. Don't top up until the first vigorous fermentation has died down. If you already have a full gallon (4.5 litres) of wine, keep some in a smaller bottle beside the demijohn and add it to the main jar later. Fit an air-lock and ferment the wine as far as it will go — it will probably stop fermenting while still sweet. If the jar is then transferred to a cool place the yeast will form a sediment very quickly.

Two rackings should give a bright, clear wine which will be ready for drinking almost at once, with a rich bouquet and a smooth, mellow, fruit flavour redolent of autumn mists. Don't add any Campden tablets if you are going to drink the wine straight away — they will only detract from the flavour.

Blackberry Wine
(Sweet)

MR NORMAN CHIVERTON OF WOOLSCOTT, WARWICKSHIRE

SECOND PRIZE, THE NATIONAL SHOW 1981

Imperial (Metric)
5 lb (2.3 kg) blackberries
  (frozen)
1 lb (450 g) elderberries
  (frozen)
½ pint (300 ml) concentrated
  red grape juice (Solvino)
2¼ lb (1 kg) sugar

American
4 lb blackberries (frozen)

1 lb elderberries (frozen)

½ pint concentrated red grape
  juice (Solvino)
1¾ lb sugar

2 tsp tartaric acid	2 tsp tartaric acid
2 tbsp premixed Bentonite suspension	2 tbsp premixed Bentonite suspension
1 tsp pectic enzyme	1 tsp pectic enzyme
1 tsp yeast nutrient (Gervin)	1 tsp yeast nutrient (Gervin)
red wine yeast (Gervin)	red wine yeast (Gervin)
water to 1 gallon (4.5 litres)	water to 1 gallon

The use of frozen fruit seems to give a better flavour and assists in the breakdown of the fruit. While waiting for the fruit to defrost, prepare a yeast starter.

Dissolve the sugar in warm water and add it to the crushed fruit in a 2-gallon (9-litre) plastic bucket with a close-fitting lid. Add all the other ingredients and mix well, then make up the volume to 5 litres. Leave to ferment for four days, stirring twice daily.

Then strain through a fine nylon sieve, without pressing hard, and place in a gallon jar fitted with cork bung and air-lock. At a temperature of about 20°C (70°F), the batch which achieved the award mentioned above fermented down to a specific gravity of 0.999 in five weeks and began to clear. It was carefully racked into another jar and 9 oz (250 g) of sugar was added to raise the specific gravity to 1.020. Sulphite and sorbate were dissolved in the wine as usual to prevent further fermentation.

Four weeks later the wine was brilliantly clear; after another racking it was kept in bulk for six months before being exhibited. It proved to be fruity, clear and stable with a very good bouquet. The wine could possibly have been kept a bit longer and may not have been sweet enough for its class. With added alcohol it would have been a port-style wine.

Blackberry Dessert Wine

MR H. WILLETT OF DANE VALLEY WINE CIRCLE

FIRST PRIZE, RED DESSERT WINE CLASS,
ICL KIDSGROVE ANNUAL SHOW 1983

Imperial (Metric)
6 lb (2.7 kg) blackberries
3½ lb (1.6 kg) sugar
pectic enzyme
yeast and nutrient
water to 1 gallon (4.5 litres)

American
5 lb blackberries
3lb sugar
pectic enzyme
yeast and nutrient
water to 1 gallon

Crush fruit in a bucket and add 5 pints (2.8 litres) of boiling water. When cool add the pectic enzyme and cover closely. Two days later add the yeast and nutrient. Leave to ferment for no longer than three days, keeping well covered and stirring three times daily.

Strain carefully on to 2 lb (900 g) of the sugar and stir to dissolve. Transfer to demijohn and fit an air-lock. The remaining sugar is dissolved in the wine a little at a time until the fermentation is complete. Rack the wine carefully off the sediment as necessary and leave for a year in bottle. A delightful wine.

Blackberry and Apple Wine
(Dry Red Table Wine)

MR SIMON SOROKA OF PLYMOUTH, DEVON

WINE OF THE SHOW, SOUTH WEST FESTIVAL OF
WINE AND BEERMAKERS 1980

Imperial (Metric)
4½ lb (2 kg) blackberries

American
3¾ lb blackberries

Imperial (Metric)	American
1 pint (550 ml) pure apple juice	*1 pint pure apple juice*
1 pint (550 ml) natural-strength red grape juice	*1 pint natural-strength red grape juice*
1½ lb (700 g) sugar	*1¼ lb sugar*
½ tsp tartaric acid	*½ tsp tartaric acid*
½ tsp citric acid	*½ tsp citric acid*
½ tsp Pectolase	*½ tsp Pectolase*
yeast and nutrient (Burgundy)	*yeast and nutrient (Burgundy)*
water to 1 gallon (4.5 litres)	*water to 1 gallon*

Wash the fruit well and place it in a fermentation bin. Add 4 pints (2.3 litres) of boiling water in which the sugar has been dissolved. When cool, crush the fruit with your (washed) hands and add 1 Campden tablet, the pectic enzyme and acids. Leave covered for two days. Then strain into a demijohn and add the yeast (as a starter) and nutrient. Fit an air-lock. When the fermentation has become less vigorous (after about four days), top up with the grape and apple juice. Allow to ferment out to dryness, then rack and store as normal.

Blackberry, Bullace and Sloe Wine
(Dry)

MR J.K. WALKER OF NEWLANDS WINE CIRCLE

FOURTH PRIZE, DRY RED FRUIT WINE CLASS,
NORTH-WEST FEDERATION SHOW

Imperial (Metric)
1¾ lb (800 g) blackberries
1 lb (450 g) bullaces
8 oz (225 g) sloes
½ pint (300 ml) concentrated red grape juice

American
1½ lb blackberries
1 ib bullaces
8 oz sloes
½ pint concentrated red grape juice

1 lb (450 g) ripe bananas	1 lb ripe bananas
1¾ lb (800 g) sugar	1½ lb sugar
pectic enzyme	pectic enzyme
yeast and nutrient (Burgundy)	yeast and nutrient (Burgundy)
water to 1 gallon (4.5 litres)	water to 1 gallon

The bullace is a wild plum, rather like a damson, and is best collected mid-September. The sloes can be gathered in late October or early November when the skins are just wrinkled. Since the fruits will be ready at different times, they can be stored in the freezer until required.

Pour about 4 pints (2.3 litres) of boiling water over the red fruit in a plastic bucket. When cool enough, crush the fruits with your (washed) hands, especially the bullaces and sloes. Simmer the bananas for thirty minutes in 2 pints (1.2 litres) of water and then strain the liquid into the bucket. Allow to cool and add the pectic enzyme. Cover and leave for twenty-four hours.

Next, dissolve the sugar in the minimum possible volume of hot water and add the resulting syrup to the bucket. When cool, add the yeast and yeast nutrient and stir well. Ferment on the pulp for five days, keeping well covered and stirring twice daily.

Then strain into a demijohn, add the grape concentrate, and top up with cool, boiled water, leaving room for frothing in the first vigorous fermentation. When the frothing has died down, top up the demijohn and ferment out to dryness. Rack off the sediment and leave to mature for at least twelve months.

The wine is similar to a Côtes du Rhone and will be around 13% alcohol by volume: "Well recommended for drinking on warm summer afternoons and at barbecues".

Blackberry and Elderberry Wine
(Dry Red Table Wine)

MR T. CORDWELL OF DERBY

WINE OF THE SHOW, LONG EATON OPEN FESTIVAL 1984

Imperial (Metric)	**American**
For 3 gallons (13.5 litres):	
6 lb (2.7 kg) blackberries (frozen)	5 lb blackberries (frozen)
3 lb (1.35 kg) elderberries (frozen)	2½ lb elderberries (frozen)
1 can (1 kg) concentrated red grape juice	1 pint concentrated red grape juice
4 lb (1.8 kg) sugar	3½ lb sugar
2 tsp grape tannin	2 tsp grape tannin
3 tsp pectic enzyme	3 tsp pectic enzyme
yeast and nutrient (Burgundy)	yeast and nutrient (Burgundy)
water to 3 gallons (13.5 litres)	water to 3 gallons

Place the frozen fruit in a 5–gallon (22.5-litre) fermentation bin and add 1 gallon (4.5 litres) of boiling water. When cool, add 3 Campden tablets, cover and leave for twenty-four hours.

Next day, add more boiling water and the concentrated grape juice. Cover and leave for twenty-four hours.

On the third day, dissolve the sugar in boiled water and add it to the fermentation bin, adjusting the volume to about 3 gallons (13.5 litres). When cool, add the grape tannin, enzyme and yeast nutrient, and mash the fruit or liquidize it with a hand–held liquidizer. Add an active yeast starter, cover and leave to ferment for two days.

Strain off the fruit pulp, return the liquid to a fermentation bin, top up to the 3-gallon (13.5-litre) level with cool, boiled water and leave for another two days. Then siphon the wine equally into three clean demijohns at normal fermentation temperature and fit air-locks.

When the fermentation has finished, rack as normal. The batch of wine which achieved the award mentioned above fermented to a specific gravity of 0.993 on the twelfth day. It was then racked into three clean demijohns and left for a further five days, after which it was racked again. It was then removed to a cold garage to clear completely and six months later it was racked once more. The wine was found to be very dry, so 3 dessertspoons of glycerine and 2 dessertspoons of lactose (an unfermentable sugar) were added to each demijohn. The wine was then matured for a further twelve months.

Blackcurrant Wine
(Dry Red Table Wine)

LOCAL WINE CIRCLE PRIZEWINNING WINE

Imperial (Metric)
1 pint (600 ml) concentrated
 red grape juice
1 can (500 ml) "Anchor"
 blackcurrant syrup★
1 lb (450 g) sugar
1 tsp citric acid
yeast and nutrient
water to 1 gallon (4.5 litres)

American
1 pint concentrated red grape
 juice
½ pint "Anchor"
 blackcurrant syrup★
12 oz sugar
1 tsp citric acid
yeast and nutrient
water to 1 gallon

★At the time of writing this brand of blackcurrant syrup contained no artificial additives or preservatives of any kind. If you use another variety which contains preservatives, simmer it in water for two or three minutes to drive off the preservative.

Prepare a yeast starter from a good variety of yeast the day before making the wine. The recipe is simplicity itself: all the ingredients are mixed together in a demijohn (ensuring the sugar is fully dissolved), the yeast is added and the fermentation is left to proceed to completion under air-lock. However, two points to note:

(i) you may find it helpful to use a hydrometer if you have one. For a dry table wine, adjust the sugar so that the s.g. of the gallon (4.5 litres) before adding yeast is about 1.080;

(ii) if you want a sweet wine, add sugar to taste when the wine is clear and stable. Alternatively you could add extra sugar to start with, aiming for an initial s.g. of, say, 1.120. However, if the yeast is a vigorous variety, it may well ferment out all the sugar and leave you with a strong, dry wine which still needs sweetening.

The wine produced in this way is fruity and delicious, with a good bouquet. It is good for drinking at once but will improve with keeping. Another advantage is that you can use one of the cheaper red grape concentrates with every hope of a good result.

Blackcurrant and Blackberry Social Wine

MR JOHN DILLEY OF SANDIACRE, NOTTINGHAMSHIRE

SECOND PRIZE, RED SOCIAL WINE CLASS,
LONG EATON OPEN FESTIVAL 1978

Imperial (Metric)
1½ lb (700 g) blackcurrants (frozen)
1½ lb (700 g) blackberries
2 lb (900 g) ripe bananas
12 oz (350 g) raisins
½ pint (300 ml) concentrated red grape juice

American
1¼ lb blackcurrants (frozen)
1¼ lb blackberries
1¾ lb ripe bananas
12 oz raisins
½ pint concentrated red grape juice

2 lb (900 g) sugar	1¾ lb sugar
pectic enzyme	pectic enzyme
2 tsp yeast nutrient	2 tsp yeast nutrient
yeast (Burgundy)	yeast (Burgundy)
water to 1 gallon (4.5 litres)	water to 1 gallon

Liquidize the blackberries, blackcurrants and peeled bananas. Mince the raisins and put them with the liquidized fruit in a fermentation bucket. Add 1¼ lb (550 g) of sugar dissolved in a little water, together with the nutrients, pectic enzyme and grape concentrate. Make the volume up to 6½ pints (3.7 litres) with water containing 1 dissolved Campden tablet. Cover and leave overnight.

Twenty-four hours later add an active yeast preparation and ferment in the bucket for five days, keeping well covered and stirring daily. Then strain the liquid into a demijohn and fit an air-lock. Keep checking the s.g. and "feed" the wine with sugar in small amounts (2 oz; 60 g) each time the s.g. falls to 1.005. When the sugar is used up (or the fermentation has finished), sweeten to s.g. 1.020 with extra sugar. Rack, stabilize and mature as normal.

Bramble Tip Wine
(Table Wine)

MR ALAN HART OF ADLINGTON WINE GUILD

SIX FIRST PRIZES IN NORTH-WEST CIRCLE SHOWS

Imperial (Metric)	**American**
4 pints (2½ litres) bramble tips	4 pints bramble tips
1 lb (450 g) sultanas	12 oz sultanas
2¼ lb (1 kg) sugar	1¾ lb sugar
1½ tsp citric acid	1½ tsp citric acid

1 tsp pectic enzyme
1 Vitamin B¹ tablet
yeast and nutrient (Sauternes)
water to 1 gallon (4.5 litres)

1 tsp pectic enzyme
1 Vitamin B¹ tablet
yeast and nutrient (Sauternes)
water to 1 gallon

1 tsp pectic enzyme
1 Vitamin B¹ tablet
yeast and nutrient (Sauternes)
water to 1 gallon (4.5 litres)

1 tsp pectic enzyme
1 Vitamin B¹ tablet
yeast and nutrient (Sauternes)
water to 1 gallon

For this lightly flavoured table wine, you will need to pick the first 2 inches (5 cm) of new bramble tips just as the buds are bursting. Wash the tips and place them in a bucket with the sugar, minced sultanas and acid. Pour on 6 pints (3.5 litres) of boiling water, cover and leave for twenty-four hours. Then add the yeast, nutrients and enzyme.

Ferment on pulp for one week, keeping well covered and stirring daily. Strain into a demijohn, top up as required, and ferment to dryness. Rack and bottle as usual.

Burnet Wine
(Dry)

MR G.A. BROWN OF CARNFORTH, LANCASHIRE

FIRST PRIZE, WARTON SHOW 1968

Imperial (Metric)
3 pints (1.7 litres) Burnet
  flower heads★
1 lb (450 g) raisins
2 lb (900 g) sugar
1 tsp tartaric acid
1 tsp pectic enzyme
1 tsp nutrient
yeast
water to 1 gallon (4.5 litres)

American
3 pints Burnet flower heads

12 oz raisins
1¾ lb sugar
1 tsp tartaric acid
1 tsp pectic enzyme
1 tsp nutrient
yeast
water to 1 gallon

★This is the Great Burnet (*Sanguisorba officinalis*) not the Burnet Rose or Salad Burnet. It grows mainly in the damp pastures and hilly meadowlands of North and Central Britain. In older days the dark crimson flower heads were used to staunch bleeding, both internally and externally — hence its name of *Sanguisorba*, which means "blood absorbing" — Ed.

Pour 2 pints (1.2 litres) of boiling water over the Burnet heads. Lightly liquidize the raisins, add 1 pint (600 ml) of boiling water, mix with the flower heads and leave overnight.

Add the yeast starter, nutrient, acid and pectic enzyme. Allow to ferment for twenty-four hours. Strain off the liquid, pressing the pulp lightly, and transfer the liquid to a demijohn. Add the sugar dissolved in enough water to bring the volume up to 1 gallon (4.5 litres). Fit an air-lock and ferment to dryness. Rack as necessary.

Carrot Wine
(Dessert or Table Wine)

ROSEBERRY WINEMAKERS' CIRCLE

PRIZEWINNING WINE, NORTH YORKSHIRE AND SOUTH DERBYSHIRE FEDERATION SHOW

Imperial (Metric)	**American**
6 lb (2.7 kg) carrots	5 lb carrots
1 lb (450 g) wheat	12 oz wheat
4 oz (110 g) raisins	4 oz raisins
2 lemons	2 lemons
2 oranges	2 oranges
sugar (see method)	sugar (see method)
1/4 tsp grape tannin	1/4 tsp grape tannin
1 tsp Pectolase	1 tsp Pectolase
1 Vitamin B^1 tablet	1 Vitamin B^1 tablet
1/2 tsp Epsom salts	1/2 tsp Epsom salts
yeast and nutrient	yeast and nutrient
water to 1 gallon (4.5 litres)	water to 1 gallon

Wash the wheat well. Put it in a basin and cover it with boiling water. Cover and leave overnight. Next day, wash the carrots, place them in a pan with 6 pints (3.5 litres) of water, bring to the boil and simmer until the carrots are very tender. Strain off the liquid and allow it to cool, then add the Pectolase and leave for at least six hours.

Put the wheat water and the strained water from the carrots into a bucket. Wash and mince the raisins and add these, together with the minced wheat, 2 lb (900 g) of sugar, and the sliced oranges and lemons. Stir until the sugar has dissolved, then add the tannin, nutrient, Epsom salts and yeast. Cover and leave to ferment on the pulp for fifteen days, stirring frequently. Then strain and put into a demijohn. Fit an air-lock and top up periodically with sugar syrup to maintain a specific gravity of 1.025–1.030. Finish at s.g. 1.030, and rack when the fermentation is finally over. Keep the containers full.

For a dry table wine, use only 8 oz (225 g) of wheat, 1 lemon, 1 orange, 4 oz (110 g) of raisins, and a total of 1 lb 12 oz (800 g) of sugar.

Chamomile Wine
(Aperitif Style)

MRS SUSAN MAKINSON OF CHORLEY WINE AND BEER CIRCLE

NORTH WEST FEDERATION SHOW PRIZEWINNING RECIPE

Imperial (Metric)
¾ oz (20 g) dried chamomile
  flowers
1 lb (450 g) sultanas
2 oranges
2 lemons
2½ lb (1.15 kg) sugar

American
½ oz dried chamomile
  flowers
12 oz sultanas
2 oranges
2 lemons
2 lb sugar

pectic enzyme
yeast and nutrient
water to 1 gallon (4.5 litres)

pectic enzyme
yeast and nutrient
water to 1 gallon

Pour 1 pint (600 ml) of boiling water onto the flowers. Cover and leave to infuse. Place the minced sultanas in a bucket with the sugar and the juice and thinly pared rind of the fruit. Pour on 6 pints (3.5 litres) of boiling water and stir until the sugar is dissolved. Cover and leave overnight.

Add the flower heads and liquid to the bucket, mix well and add a yeast starter and nutrient preparation. Ferment in the bucket for seven days, keeping well covered and stirring twice daily.

Strain out the solids and transfer the liquid to a demijohn. Top up if necessary, fit an air-lock and ferment until dry or medium dry. Stabilize the wine with sorbate and 1 Campden tablet in the normal way; rack, and bottle when the wine is perfectly clear.

Cherry Dessert Wine

MR W.E. GRAINGER OF SHIRLEY, SURREY

FIRST PRIZE, THE NATIONAL SHOW 1985

Imperial (Metric)
6 lb (2.7 kg) very ripe black
    cherries
1 lb (450 g) very ripe morello
    cherries
6 oz (170 g) concentrated red
    grape juice
sugar (see method)
1 tsp citric acid

American
5 lb very ripe black cherries

12 oz very ripe morello
    cherries
6 oz concentrated red grape
    juice
sugar (see method)
1 tsp citric acid

<table>
<tr><td>1 tsp nutrient</td><td>1 tsp nutrient</td></tr>
<tr><td>1 tsp pectic enzyme</td><td>1 tsp pectic enzyme</td></tr>
<tr><td>yeast (preferably Gervin Number 3)</td><td>yeast (preferably Gervin Number 3)</td></tr>
<tr><td>water to 1 gallon (4.5 litres)</td><td>water to 1 gallon</td></tr>
</table>

1 tsp nutrient
1 tsp pectic enzyme
yeast (preferably Gervin
 Number 3)
water to 1 gallon (4.5 litres)

1 tsp nutrient
1 tsp pectic enzyme
yeast (preferably Gervin
 Number 3)
water to 1 gallon

Prepare a starter bottle using ½ pint (300 ml) of cool, boiled water, 1 tbsp sugar, the acid, nutrient and yeast. Plug the jar with cotton wool or kitchen paper and leave overnight at about 20°C (70°F). At the same time, stone the cherries, place them in a plastic fermentation bin or bucket and cover with 4 pints (2.3 litres) of cool, boiled water. Add the pectic enzyme and 1 crushed Campden tablet. Stir, cover and leave overnight.

Next morning add the yeast starter and 1 lb (450 g) of the sugar dissolved in a little water to the cherries. Stir well, cover and leave to ferment for four days, stirring daily. Then strain into a demijohn and top up to the 6 pint (3.5 litre) level. Fit an air-lock and leave to ferment at 20°C (70°F). Add the remainder of the sugar in small amounts as necessary to keep the fermentation going. Up to 3 lb (1.35 kg) of sugar will be absorbed before the yeast ceases to work. Ensure the sugar is dissolved thoroughly and mixed well into the bulk after each addition. Try to finish the wine dry for storage.

When the fermentation has finished, rack the wine, top up the demijohn with a similar wine and add 1 crushed Campden tablet. It is then stored for one year in a cool (13°–15°C, 55°–60°F) dark place, sealed with a cork bung.

After twelve months the wine can be tasted, and the balance adjusted by the addition of about ½ pint (300 ml) of a high fruit and alcohol content elderberry wine made in a similar way. (In both cases the fruit must be very ripe to avoid excess acidity.) Similarly, the amount of sugar needed to give the desired degree of sweetness also varies, but about 8 oz (225 g) dissolved in a portion of the wine and then well mixed in is usually sufficient. The adjusted wine is returned to store for at least two more years before drinking or showing.

Note: After straining the must into the bucket, a second batch of 1 gallon (4.5 litres) can be made from the fruit pulp. Add 2 lb (900 g) of sugar, 7 pints (4.0 litres) of cool, boiled water and 1 tsp of nutrients. Allow this to ferment for a further three days before straining into a demijohn, then top up and ferment as normal. This second run of rich red wine will mature far more quickly than the first — and should protect the "star of the piece" from premature depredations!

Cherry and Blackcurrant Wine
(Sweet)

MR GEORGE SIMMONS OF TUDELEY, KENT

FIRST PRIZE, LANGTON GREEN OPEN SHOW 1986

Imperial (Metric)
3 lb (1.35 kg) morello cherries
  (fresh or canned)
2 lb (900 g) black dessert
  cherries
1 lb (450 g) blackcurrants
½ pint (300 ml) concentrated
  red grape juice
3 ripe bananas
2¾ lb (1.25 kg) sugar
½ tsp grape tannin
1 tsp tartaric acid
1 tsp pectic enzyme
1 tsp glycerine
yeast (Port) and nutrient
water to 1 gallon (4.5 litres)

American
2½ lb morello cherries (fresh
  or canned)
1¾ lb black dessert cherries

1 lb blackcurrants
½ pint concentrated red grape
  juice
3 ripe bananas
2¼ lb sugar
½ tsp grape tannin
1 tsp tartaric acid
1 tsp pectic enzyme
1 tsp glycerine
yeast (Port) and nutrient
water to 1 gallon

Wash the fruit (except the bananas) and place it in a mashing bin or bucket together with 5 pints (2.8 litres) of cold water. Mash gently, so as to ensure that no stones are broken, and add the tannin, pectic enzyme and 1 crushed Campden tablet. Cover and leave for twenty-four hours. Next day simmer three ripe, peeled, chopped bananas in 1 pint (600 ml) of water for ten minutes and add the resulting "juice" to the fermentation bin. Discard the solids. Allow to cool then add the yeast, nutrient, grape concentrate and ½ tsp of Bentonite finings. Ferment on the pulp for five days, keeping well covered and stirring twice daily.

Strain off the fruit and dissolve 2 lb (900 g) of sugar in the liquid. Pour into a demijohn and fit an air-lock. Add the remaining sugar in three equal amounts each time the specific gravity falls to 1.030. Finally, when the s.g. has fallen to about 1.020, rack into a clean demijohn and terminate fermentation with a Campden tablet and the recommended amount of a stabilizer such as potassium sorbate. At this stage the wine may be topped up with natural-strength (not concentrated) red grape juice.

Rack as necessary. After the final racking, add 10 drops of almond essence and 1 tsp of glycerine.

Crab Apple Wine
(Dry)

MR JOHN COTTERELL OF WOLVERHAMPTON WINEMAKERS' CIRCLE

Imperial (Metric)
For 3 gallons (14 litres):
12 lb (5.4 kg) crab apples★
  (Aldenham Purple)
sugar (see method)
pectic enzyme

American
10 lb crab apples★ (Aldenham
  Purple)
sugar (see method)
pectic enzyme

yeast and nutrient
2 gallons (9 litres) water

yeast and nutrient
2 gallons water

*Any red or red-and-green coloured crab apple can be used to make wine, but avoid the green sort, which are extremely acidic — Ed.

The suburban roads around Wolverhampton were planted some years ago with a decorative *Malus* species known as Aldenham Purple. The trees are now full grown and bear apples about the size of a medium Worcester, with dark scarlet skins, a colour which stains the pulp. Mr Cotterell has made up to 40 gallons (200 litres) of wine a year from these apples, always using a delightfully simple method.

The apples are minced whole into 2 gallons (9 litres) of water, the other ingredients are added and the must is then fermented on the pulp for seven days. The liquid is then strained off, 2½ lb (1.15 kg) of sugar is dissolved in each gallon (4.5 litres) of juice, and the fermentation is continued under air-lock until complete. The wine is racked when clear; one then has about 3 gallons (14 litres) of delightful dry wine.

Crab Apple Wine
(Medium Table Wine)

MR J.K. WALKER OF NEWLANDS WINE CIRCLE

SECOND PRIZE, WHITE OR GOLDEN MEDIUM TABLE WINE CLASS,
NORTH-WEST FEDERATION SHOW 1985

Imperial (Metric)
6 lb (2.7 kg) crab apples
    (John Downie)*
2¼ lb (1 kg) sugar
6 drops liquid tannin
pectic enzyme
yeast (Sauternes) and nutrient

American
5 lb crab apples (John
    Downie)*
1¾ lb sugar
6 drops liquid tannin
pectic enzyme
yeast (Sauternes) and nutrient

water to 1 gallon (4.5 litres)   *water to 1 gallon*

*John Downie are the variety usually recommended, but Aldenham Purple or Bradmore can be used — Ed.

Wash the apples thoroughly, cut into small pieces and immediately transfer to a bucket containing 4 pints (2.3 litres) of cold water in which a Campden tablet has been dissolved. This is important to avoid browning of the apples. Add pectic enzyme to the bucket, cover and leave for seven days, stirring daily.

Strain the liquid into a demijohn, add the tannin, yeast, nutrient and the sugar dissolved in enough water to bring the volume up to 1 gallon (4.5 litres). Ferment to dryness.

When fermentation has finished the wine can be racked and bottled. Add sugar syrup to taste immediately before drinking. Ready at six months but will keep for several years.

Damson Wine
(Dry)

MR A.L. KEE OF ROUNDHOUSE WINE CIRCLE

THIRD PRIZE, DRY RED FRUIT WINE CLASS,
ROUNDHOUSE WINE CIRCLE SHOW 1984

Imperial (Metric)
*4 lb (1.8 kg) damsons (fresh
  or canned)*
8 oz (225 g) currants
*1/3 pint (200 ml) concentrated
  red grape juice*
1¾ lb (800 g) sugar
pectic enzyme
yeast and nutrient
water to 1 gallon (4.5 litres)

American
*3½ lb damsons (fresh or
  canned)*
8 oz currants
*1/3 pint concentrated red grape
  juice*
1½ lb sugar
pectic enzyme
yeast and nutrient
water to 1 gallon

The secret of making good damson wine is to pick fruit that is really ripe. This, unfortunately, is often hard to obtain in Britain! Because of the variation in the fruit's acidity it is helpful to check and adjust the acid if you can, although not essential.

Wash the currants and damsons in hot water. Then place both these fruits in a pan with about 5 pints (2.8 litres) of water and heat gently to boiling point. Cover and leave to cool, then transfer to a fermentation bucket and add the remaining ingredients; it is helpful to dissolve the sugar in water before adding it to the bucket. Check the temperature is correct and introduce a yeast starter. Top up the volume to around the gallon mark (4.5 litres). Cover and leave to ferment on the pulp for two or three days, stirring twice daily.

Strain the must carefully into a fermentation jar. You should exclude as much fruit pulp as you can, so do not press the straining bag. It simply isn't worth getting fruit pulp into the demijohn, since this so often spoils the flavour of a wine.

Fit an air-lock and ferment to completion. The wine will begin to clear very quickly if transferred to a cool place, and can then be racked. Add 1 Campden tablet and top up as necessary with water. Leave to clear, rack again, then store for about a year before sampling. If the wine is too dry, a little sugar may be dissolved in each bottle, a teaspoonful or less at a time, until the wine is sweet enough for your palate.

Damson Dessert Wine

FIRST PRIZE, RED DESSERT WINE CLASS,
LOCAL WINE CIRCLE SHOW 1985

Imperial (Metric)
6 lb (2.7 kg) fresh, ripe
    damsons

American
5 lb fresh, ripe damsons

1 can (1 kg) port-type concentrate	1 pint port-type concentrate
sugar (see method)	sugar (see method)
2 tsp tartaric acid	2 tsp tartaric acid
pectic enzyme	pectic enzyme
1 fl oz (30 ml) glycerol	1 fl oz glycerol
yeast and nutrient (including Vitamin B^1)	yeast and nutrient (including Vitamin B^1)
water to 1 gallon (4.5 litres)	water to 1 gallon

Bring the damsons up to boiling point in 6 pints (3.5 litres) of water and simmer for four or five minutes. Mash gently, allow to cool, then strain through a fine mesh into a fermentation bucket. Add the remaining ingredients, following the instructions on the can of concentrate for the addition of sugar. Mix well, make up to the gallon (4.5 litres) and leave to ferment for three days with a lid on at normal fermentation temperature (20°C/70°F).

Transfer to a demijohn and fit an air-lock. Top up when you have added the sugar as instructed and you are sure there will not be an overflow from a vigorous fermentation. If you have a hydrometer you can add a little extra sugar in 2-oz lots each time the specific gravity falls to 1.005.

When the fermentation has finally ended, rack off the sediment and add a Campden tablet. The wine can be left to clear but may well need fining. Add the glycerol and check the sweetness before storing the wine in bulk for about one year, racking every four months to assist the wine's maturation.

Damson and Elderberry Wine
(Dry Red Table Wine)

FYLDE AMATEUR WINEMAKERS' GUILD
FIRST PRIZE, TAWD VALE OPEN SHOW 1975

Imperial (Metric)
8 oz (225 g) canned damsons (stoned)
½ can elderberry juice
8 oz (225 g) sultanas
8 oz (225 g) peeled bananas
1¾ lb (800 g) sugar
½ tsp tartaric acid
1 Vitamin B¹ tablet
1 tsp Pectolase
1 tsp nutrient
yeast starter (general-purpose)
water to 1 gallon (4.5 litres)

American
8 oz canned damsons (stoned)
8 oz canned elderberry juice
8 oz sultanas
8 oz peeled bananas
1½ lb sugar
½ tsp tartaric acid
1 Vitamin B¹ tablet
1 tsp Pectolase
1 tsp nutrient
yeast starter (general-purpose)
water to 1 gallon

Chop the sultanas and place them in a 2-gallon (9 litre) plastic bucket with 2 pints (1.2 litres) of boiling water. Add the "juice" obtained by simmering the chopped bananas in 1 pint (600 ml) of water for thirty minutes. Add the sugar, damsons and elderberry juice and stir to ensure the sugar dissolves completely. Make up to 1 gallon (4.5 litres) with cool, boiled water, then add the pectic enzyme, acid, nutrients and yeast. Stir well. Cover with a cloth and leave in a warm place for seven days, stirring daily.

Next, strain through a nylon bag into a 1-gallon (4.5-litre) jar, top up with cool, boiled water and fit an air-lock. Leave to ferment out, then rack off and dissolve 1 Campden tablet and 1 sorbate tablet in the wine. One month later, rack again and filter if necessary. Bottle and mature as appropriate.

Elderberry Wine
(Dry Table Wine)

MR DON SAYERS OF PEASMARSH, EAST SUSSEX

Imperial (Metric)
4 lb (1.8 kg) elderberries
    (stripped from stalks)
2½ lb (1.15 kg) sugar
4 oz (110 g) raisins
1 Vitamin B[1] tablet
1 tsp pectic enzyme
1 tsp yeast nutrient
yeast
water to 1 gallon (4.5 litres)

American
3½ lb elderberries (stripped
    from stalks)
2 lb sugar
4 oz raisins
1 Vitamin B[1] tablet
1 tsp pectic enzyme
1 tsp yeast nutrient
yeast
water to 1 gallon

Put the elderberries and the roughly chopped raisins into a suitable pan with 6½ pints (3.7 litres) of cold water. Heat slowly until just below boiling point, then turn off the heat and leave for about five minutes for juice to leave the berries. Strain through a coarse straining bag into a plastic bucket and add the sugar. Stir well to dissolve. When the must has reached fermentation temperature (20°C/70°F), add the yeast, nutrient and Vitamin B[1]. A 20 mg Vitamin C tablet may also be added at this stage as a precaution against oxidation. Cover and ferment for three days before straining into a fermentation jar. Top up, fit an air-lock and ferment out in the normal way.

When the fermentation is complete, rack into a clean jar and dissolve 2 Campden tablets in the wine. Transfer to a cool place for about nine months, then rack again and add about two or three teaspoons of powdered gelatine. This will ensure that the tannin is eliminated.

Leave for a further three months, then rack again before drinking the wine or laying it down.

Elderberry Wine
(Dry Table Wine)

MR RON FOLLEY OF WYTHENSHAWE WINE SOCIETY

SECOND PRIZE, DRY RED TABLE WINE CLASS,
NORTH-WEST FEDERATION SHOW 1985

Imperial (Metric)

For 5 gallons (22.5 litres):
12 lb (5.4 kg) elderberries (frozen)
1 lb (450 g) sultanas (chopped)
1 lb (450 g) dried morello cherries★
3½ pints (2 litres) pure apple juice
¾ pint (500 ml) natural-strength red grape juice
2 cans (2 kg) concentrated red grape juice
9 lb (4 kg) sugar
5 Vitamin B¹ tablets
Gervin Number 2 yeast
water to 5 gallons (22.5 litres)

American

10 lb elderberries (frozen)
12 oz sultanas (chopped)
12 oz dried morello cherries★
3½ pints pure apple juice
¾ pint natural-strength red grape juice
2 pints concentrated red grape juice
7½ lb sugar
5 Vitamin B¹ tablets
Gervin Number 2 yeast
water to 5 gallons

★Approximately equal to 4 lb (1.8 kg) of fresh cherries which are a suitable alternative — Ed.

Place the elderberries, sultanas and cherries in a steam juice extractor. Transfer the resulting juice to a fermentation vessel and add three quarters of the sugar (as syrup), the concentrate, grape juice and Vitamin B¹. Make the volume up to 4 gallons (18 litres) with water and add the yeast.

Ferment the wine until the specific gravity falls to about 1.002, then add the remaining sugar (as syrup) and the apple juice. Continue the fermentation to dryness, and rack and sulphite in the normal way. The batch which achieved the award mentioned above fermented out to s.g. 0.992 and contained 12% alcohol by volume.

As a bonus, the residue of the fruit pulp was used to produce another gallon (4.5 litres) of wine with the addition of 2¼ lb (1 kg) of sugar. No extra yeast was needed.

Elderberry Wine
(Dry Full-Bodied Red Wine)

MR ALLEN HAMBLETON OF SHEFFIELD

FIRST PRIZE, SOUTH YORKSHIRE AND NORTH DERBYSHIRE ASSOCIATION OF WINE GUILDS SHOW

Imperial (Metric)

For 5 gallons (22.5 litres):
10 lb (4.6 kg) fresh or frozen
   elderberries
7½ lb (3.45 kg) ripe or
   overripe bananas
7½ lb (3.45 kg) Bramley
   apples
   or 5 pints (3 litres) pure
   apple juice
2½ cans (2.5 kg)
   concentrated red grape juice
7½ lb (3.45 kg) sugar
4 tsp dried grape tannin
   powder
pectic enzyme
yeast (Red wine) and nutrient
water to 5 gallons (22.5 litres)

American

8 lb fresh or frozen
   elderberries
6 lb ripe or overripe bananas

6 lb Bramley apples

   or 5 pints pure apple juice

2½ pints concentrated red
   grape juice
6 lb sugar
4 tsp dried grape tannin
   powder
pectic enzyme
yeast (Red wine) and nutrient
water to 5 gallons

The quality of the elderberries is of prime importance, so ensure when picking them that they are fully black, ripe and sweet. They must not taste woody and unripe. Remove the berries from the stalks and wash them thoroughly in a large bin or bucket, letting the berries sink and settle on the bottom before skimming off any leaves and unripe berries which are floating on the surface. Strain off the water and transfer the berries to a clean container. At this stage, if you wish, the berries may be frozen until it is convenient to make the wine. Freezing certainly helps to extract the juice, but it is not essential.

Crush the berries and strain off the juice into a 6-gallon (30-litre) fermentation bin. Place the elderberry pulp into a boiler or several large pans and add 2 gallons (9 litres) of water. Bring to the boil and simmer for ten to fifteen minutes. Strain and press out the "juice", adding it to the juice already placed in the fermentation bin. Discard the pulp.

Peel and slice the bananas, and boil them (without the skins) for thirty minutes in 1½ gallons (7 litres) of water. Strain off the liquid, add it to the elderberry juice, and discard the pulp. Dissolve all the sugar in the hot liquid and add the tannin. Top up with cold water if necessary to 4¼ gallons (19 litres). When the must is at normal fermentation temperature, add the pectic enzyme, nutrient and an active yeast starter. At this stage the apples are also incorporated into the procedure. For best results, the fresh apples can be washed and liquidized, before being fermented separately for three to four days in about 1 gallon (4.5 litres) of the fermenting elderberry juice; the smaller quantity of liquid makes pressing out the juice easier. Alternatively, 5 pints (3 litres) of pure apple juice may be mixed in at once, with quite good results and a lot less fuss than the fresh apples. Keep the fermentation vessels covered.

After about five days, when the first vigorous fermentation is slowing down, add the red grape concentrate and then leave the wine to ferment to completion under an air-lock before racking. Rack again when the wine is clear, and add the equivalent of 1 Campden tablet per gallon at each of these two rackings. Leave undisturbed for at least one year.

Dried Elderberry Wine
(Table Wine)

MR BRIAN KEER OF NEWQUAY, CORNWALL

FIRST PRIZE, THREE WINES FOR A DINNER CLASS,
SOUTH-WESTERN COUNTIES WINE AND BEERMAKERS'
FEDERATION FESTIVAL 1981

Imperial (Metric)
8 oz (225 g) dried elderberries
4 oz (110 g) seedless raisins
6 oz (170 g) peeled bananas
¼ pint (150 ml) concentrated
  red grape juice (CWE)
2 lb (900 g) sugar
1 tsp acid blend
  (citric, tartaric, malic)
1 tsp Tronozymol nutrient
1 Vitamin B¹ tablet
pectic enzyme
Burgundy yeast (Unican)
water to 1 gallon (4.5 litres)

American
8 oz dried elderberries
4 oz seedless raisins
6 oz peeled bananas
¼ pint concentrated red grape
  juice (CWE)
1¾ lb sugar
1 tsp acid blend
  (citric, tartaric, malic)
1 tsp Tronozymol nutrient
1 Vitamin B¹ tablet
pectic enzyme
Burgundy yeast (Unican)
water to 1 gallon

Prepare a yeast starter the day before making the wine.

Rinse the raisins with boiling water then mince them. Place them with the dried elderberries and sugar in a fermentation bin or bucket and pour 4 pints (2.3 litres) of boiling water over them. Peel the bananas, cut into slices, and simmer for fifteen minutes in 2 pints (1.2 litres) of water. Add only the liquid to the fruit in the bucket. Cover and allow to cool to

20°C (70°F), then add the acid, nutrients and pectic enzyme. A pinch of Epsom salts may also be added at this stage (if available). Ferment on the pulp for three days, keeping covered and stirring twice daily.

Strain into a gallon (4.5-litre) jar and add the grape juice concentrate. Mix well, then top up to the shoulder with cool, boiled water. The jar can be topped up to the neck when the initial vigorous fermentation has subsided. Ferment to completion under an air-lock, then rack off the sediment, add a Campden tablet and top up with a similar dry red wine or cool, boiled water.

Rack once more in two months' time, and again four months after that. Bottle at one year. The wine should be an excellent dry, vinous table wine with a deep Burgundy colour.

[The two accompanying wines were Mr Keer's Apple Dry Table Wine and his Bilberry, Elderberry and Blackberry Dessert Wine, both of which are included in this book — Ed.]

Elderberry Wine
(Sweet)

MR G. ROTHERHAM OF SOUTHPORT WINE CIRCLE

BEST SWEET WINE IN SHOW, GOLDEN SHOW OF THE NORTH 1980

Imperial (Metric)
4 lb (1.8 kg) elderberries
2 lb (900 g) bananas
4 oz (110 g) raisins
1 cooking apple
2½ lb (1.15 kg) sugar
1 lb (450 g) honey
pectic enzyme
yeast (Burgundy) and nutrient
water to 1 gallon (4.5 litres)

American
3½ lb elderberries
1¾ lb bananas
4 oz raisins
1 cooking apple
2 lb sugar
12 oz honey
pectic enzyme
yeast (Burgundy) and nutrient
water to 1 gallon

Place the elderberries, minced raisins, honey, sugar and the chopped apple in a plastic fermentation bin. Then pour on the liquid obtained by gently simmering the bananas in 3 pints (1.7 litres) of water for fifteen minutes. Mash the fruit and add boiling water to bring the volume up to 1 gallon (4.5 litres). Stir well to dissolve the honey and sugar. Cover and allow the must to cool.

Next day add an active yeast starter and the nutrient. Stir well, cover and leave to ferment for two days, stirring daily. Strain into a gallon demijohn and allow to ferment out. Rack and top up as normal. The wine can be stabilized with sulphite and sorbate if necessary. Best left for two years to mature.

Elderberry Wine
(Sweet)

MR VINCENT CROOK OF PRESTON WINEMAKERS' CIRCLE

Imperial (Metric)	**American**
For 5 gallons (22.5 litres):	
15 lb (7 kg) ripe elderberries	12½ lb ripe elderberries
15 lb (7 kg) sugar	12½ lb sugar
5 tsp citric acid	5 tsp citric acid
3 tsp Pectolase	3 tsp Pectolase
5 Vitamin B¹ tablets	5 Vitamin B¹ tablets
10 tsp Tronozymol nutrient	10 tsp Tronozymol nutrient
Port-type yeast (Unican)	Port-type yeast (Unican)
water to 5 gallons (22.5 litres)	water to 5 gallons

Strip the berries by hand into a bowl until the necessary weight has been collected. Wash them in cold water, then transfer them to a large fermentation bin and crush them. Add all the sugar and the acid, and pour on 25–30 pints (14–16 litres) of boiling water. When the fruit and liquid have cooled to

20–25°C (70–75°F), add the nutrients, Pectolase and a starter bottle of port yeast which was prepared beforehand. Cover the mixture and ferment on the pulp for four days; it is important not to exceed this, or the wine will contain excess tannin. Stir twice daily.

Strain off into an ex-wine 5-gallon (22.5-litre) plastic container, making the volume up to 5 gallons (22.5 litres). Fit an air-lock and leave to ferment out. When the fermentation is complete, rack the wine off the sediment and return it to the cleaned container; keep it in a cool place. Rack the wine every six months or so for eighteen months to two years.

Then sweeten the wine with sugar syrup as required and transfer it to five demijohns. The wine can then remain undisturbed until one needs it for sampling or showing. As Mr Crook observes: "This is a superb wine, but it does need time to mature. Despite the fact that the recipe uses neither raisins nor grape concentrate, the wine has vinosity. And wherever it has been entered in a show it has won an award — First, Second or Third. It is so simple to make, and just needs time and patience."

Elderberry Dessert Wine

MR V.H. GOFFEN OF PETERSFIELD, HAMPSHIRE

FIRST PRIZE, THE NATIONAL SHOW

Imperial (Metric)
4 lb (1.8 kg) ripe elderberries
1 lb (450 g) damsons (fresh or canned)
1 can (1 kg) concentrated red grape juice (Solvino Italian Classic)
sugar (see method)

American
3½ lb ripe elderberries
1 lb damsons (fresh or canned)

1 pint concentrated red grape juice (Solvino Italian Classic)
sugar (see method)

¹/3 tsp tartaric acid
²/3 tsp citric acid
Rohament P
1 oz (30 g) Bentonite
yeast (Burgundy) and nutrient
water to 1 gallon (4.5 litres)

¹/3 tsp tartaric acid
²/3 tsp citric acid
Rohament P
1 oz Bentonite
yeast (Burgundy) and nutrient
water to 1 gallon

Scald all the fruit (but do not boil it) and leave it to soak overnight in hot water. Prepare the yeast starter bottle. Next day, squash the fruit and add the Bentonite, Rohament P and 1 Campden tablet. Stir frequently, otherwise keeping covered; strain after seventy-two hours.

Add the grape concentrate, nutrients and acids to the strained fruit juices. Next, add enough sugar to produce a total volume of just under 1 gallon (4.5 litres) and a specific gravity of about 1.140. (Invert the sugar by boiling it with some of the acid before adding it to the liquor.) Pour everything into a demijohn and add the yeast starter. Do not top up until the initial vigorous fermentation has slowed down, and remember to top up with syrup whose specific gravity is about 1.140. Conduct the fermentation under air-lock at 18–21°C (65–70°F).

Rack the wine off the sediment when fermentation stops; do not delay this. Add a Campden tablet to the wine and check the specific gravity. It should be about 1.025. If it is lower (as it may be with a good yeast, giving about 18% alcohol), add sugar until this figure is reached. One ounce (30 g) of sugar will raise the specific gravity by about 0.002. Rack the wine off the sediment again one month later, and keep it in bulk for one year before bottling. Do not drink before the following year.

Elderberry and Raisin Wine
(Dry Table Wine)

MR PETER WITHERDEN OF POOLE, DORSET

LOCAL CIRCLE PRIZEWINNING WINE

Imperial (Metric)
4 oz (110 g) dried elderberries
8 oz (225 g) raisins
1 lb.(450 g) overripe bananas
2¼ lb (1 kg) sugar
tartaric acid (as required)
1 Vitamin B¹ tablet
pectic enzyme
yeast and nutrient
water to 1 gallon (4.5 litres)

American
4 oz dried elderberries
8 oz raisins
1 lb overripe bananas
1¾ lb sugar
tartaric acid (as required)
1 Vitamin B¹ tablet
pectic enzyme
yeast and nutrient
water to 1 gallon

Thoroughly wash the raisins and elderberries. Soak the raisins in hot water until they have swollen, then strain off the water and discard it; mince the raisins. Meanwhile, peel and slice the bananas and boil the slices in 2 pints (1.2 litres) of water for thirty minutes. Add the resulting "juice" to the elderberries in a fermentation bucket and allow to cool. Then add the minced raisins, pectic enzyme and 1 crushed Campden tablet. Stir well and cover. Make up a yeast starter bottle and leave both starter and must in a warm place until the following day.

Next day make the must up to 6 pints (3.5 litres) with tap water and add the nutrients and acid, adjusting the acidity to 4 p.p.t. Dissolve the sugar in 1 pint (600 ml) of boiling water; when the solution has cooled add it to the must. If you have a hydrometer adjust the s.g. to 1.080. Ensure the must is at fermentation temperature (20–25°C/70–75°) and pitch in the yeast from the starter bottle. Stir and cover. Ferment on the pulp for three days at 25°C (75°F) stirring twice daily.

Strain through fine muslin or sieve into a sterile demijohn. Top up with tap water and ferment to dryness under an air-lock. Carry out the usual racking procedure as required, but add only one more Campden tablet, about one month before bottling. Allow the wine to mature for three months in bottle, in a cool place, ideally at a temperature of 12°C (50°F), before drinking.

Elderberry and Rosehip Wine
(Dry Table Wine)

MR DON SAYERS OF PEASMARSH, EAST SUSSEX

Imperial (Metric)
For 4 gallons (18 litres):
2 × 15 oz cans (900 g) "Irish" elderberry juice
1 × 15 oz can (450 g) "Irish" rosehip purée
1 lb (450 g) bananas
1 can (1 kg) concentrated red grape juice (CWE)
5 lb (2.3 kg) sugar
2 tsp grape tannin
2 Vitamin B¹ tablets
pectic enzyme
yeast (general-purpose) and nutrient
water to 4 gallons (18 litres)

American
2 lb "Irish" elderberry juice (canned)
1 lb "Irish" rosehip purée (canned)
1 lb bananas
1 pint concentrated red grape juice (CWE)
4 lb sugar
2 tsp grape tannin
2 Vitamin B¹ tablets
pectic enzyme
yeast (general-purpose) and nutrient
water to 4 gallons

Peel the bananas and discard the skins. Cut the fruit into slices and simmer for fifteen to twenty minutes in 1 pint (600 ml) of water. Strain and add the liquid to the elderberry juice, rosehip purée, grape concentrate and nutrients. (Three or four

20 mg Vitamin C tablets may also be dissolved in the wine at this stage as a precaution against oxidation or browning.) Next add the sugar and enough water to make the volume up to 3½ gallons (16 litres). Aim for a specific gravity of 1.080 or 1.085 before adding the yeast. Cover the fermentation bin and leave to ferment at 25°C (75°F) for three days. Then strain carefully into four 1-gallon demijohns and fit air-locks. The demijohns can be topped up to the gallon (4.5 litre) level when the first vigorous fermentation has slowed down.

There should be no difficulty in achieving a dry wine with a final s.g. in the region of 0.990. Rack into clean jars and add 2 Campden tablets per gallon (4.5 litres). Keep cool for one year and then adjust the acid and tannin if necessary.

Elderflower Wine
(Sweet)

MRS B. WATSON OF NEWLANDS WINE CIRCLE

GOLD MEDAL WINNER, THE NATIONAL SHOW 1984

Imperial (Metric)
1 pint (600 ml) elderflowers★
  (not pressed down)
12 oz (350 g) raisins
1 orange
2 lemons
3 lb (1.35 kg) sugar
1 tsp grape tannin
pectic enzyme
yeast and nutrient
water to 1 gallon (4.5 litres)

American
1 pint elderflowers★ (not
  pressed down)
12 oz raisins
1 orange
2 lemons
2½ lb sugar
1 tsp grape tannin
pectic enzyme
yeast and nturient
water to 1 gallon

★An alternative would be to use ½ oz (15 g) of dried elderflowers, infusing them in hot water. Alternatively, they can be soaked in 6 pints (3.5 litres) of cold water in which 1 Campden tablet had been dissolved. In the latter case add the yeast etc., twenty-four hours later — Ed.

Put the elderflowers in a fermentation bin and pour on 6 pints (3.5 litres) of boiling water in which the sugar has been dissolved. Stir well. Chop the raisins and add them to the bucket, together with the juice and thinly pared skin of the orange and lemons. Allow to cool, then add yeast and nutrient.

Leave to ferment for five days, keeping well covered and stirring daily. Strain into a demijohn, make up the volume to 1 gallon (4.5 litres) and leave until fermentation has finished. Rack now, adding 1 Campden tablet, and again when the wine is clear. Allow to mature for about two months before bottling.

[When making elderflower wine, it is important to choose only the pleasantly scented cream or white flowers, and to process them on the day they are picked — Ed.]

Folly (Vine Prunings) Wine
(Medium Dry White Table Wine)

MRS SUSAN OLFORD OF YAPTON, WEST SUSSEX

HIGHLY COMMENDED, MEDIUM DRY WHITE TABLE WINE CLASS, THE NATIONAL SHOW 1985

Imperial (Metric)	**American**
2 gallon bucketful (9 litres) vine prunings (lightly pressed down)	2 gallons vine prunings (lightly pressed down)
½ pint (300 ml) concentrated white grape juice	½ pint concentrated white grape juice
1 lemon (small)	1 lemon (small)
1¾ lb (800 g) sugar	1½ lb sugar
½ tsp tartaric acid	½ tsp tartaric acid
1 Vitamin B1 tablet	1 Vitamin B1 tablet
2 tsp nutrient	2 tsp nutrient
yeast (Gervin Number 1)	yeast (Gervin Number 1)
water to 1 gallon (4.5 litres)	water to 1 gallon

Put vine prunings (picked at the end of July) into a bucket with 4 pints (2.3 litres) of water, and add the lemon juice, 1 dissolved Campden tablet and 1 tsp of Bentonite (previously mixed according to instructions on packet). Cover and leave to soak, stirring twice daily, for three days.

Strain off the liquid into a 1-gallon (4.5-litre) demijohn. Leave to stand overnight, if wished, to rack off deposit. Return liquid to demijohn and add the grape concentrate, tartaric acid and nutrients, being careful to ensure all are dissolved. Next, dissolve the sugar in 1½ pints (850 ml) of warm water and add the solution to the demijohn, topping up with cold water to the gallon (4.5 litre) level. The starting gravity of the batch of wine which won the prize mentioned below was 1.080.

Allow fermentation to proceed at 18°C (65°F) under air-lock until the required specific gravity is achieved. (The batch of wine in question was fermented to an s.g. of 1.002.) Stabilize with Campden tablets and sorbate in accordance with the manufacturer's instructions. Rack and mature as normal, fining or filtering if wished. Store in a dark place to avoid browning. This wine was exhibited when nine months old.

Goldenrod Wine
(Sweet)

MRS K.M. SUTCLIFFE OF TODMORDEN WINE CIRCLE

FIRST PRIZE, TODMORDEN SHOW

Imperial (Metric)
*1 pint (600 ml) Goldenrod★
(blossom only)*
8 oz (225 g) sultanas
6 sweet oranges
3½ lb (1.6 kg) sugar
2 tsp Tronozymol nutrient

American
*1 pint Goldenrod★ (blossom
only)*
8 oz sultanas
6 sweet oranges
3 lb sugar
2 tsp Tronozymol nutrient

1 tsp citric acid	*1 tsp citric acid*
yeast	*yeast*
water to 1 gallon (4.5 litres)	*water to 1 gallon*

*Goldenrod grows among the rocks of upland Britain. Its recorded history begins in sixteenth-century London where the plant was much in demand as a herb for healing wounds caused by sword fights. In fact its Latin name *Solidago virgaurea* comes from the Latin verb "solidare", which means "to make whole or heal". It was applied externally as an ointment or drunk as a hot beverage — Ed.

Dissolve the sugar in boiling water and pour over the flowers. Add the grated peel from three of the oranges and the juice of all six. Allow to cool and then add a prepared yeast starter, nutrient and acid. Leave to ferment for four days, keeping well covered and stirring twice daily. Strain into a fermentation jar with air-lock, and leave to ferment to desired degree of sweetness. Stabilize and rack as normal, repeating when necessary. Store for several months before use.

Gooseberry Wine
(Dry)

MR NORMAN CHIVERTON OF WOOLSCOTT, WARWICKSHIRE

BEST OVERALL WINE, DRY WHITE OR GOLDEN FRUIT WINE CLASS, NATIONAL SHOW 1984

Imperial (Metric)	**American**
4 lb (1.8 kg) frozen gooseberries★	*3½ lb frozen gooseberries★*
1 pint (550 ml) concentrated white grape juice (Solvino)	*1 pint concentrated white grape juice (Solvino)*
sugar (see method)	*sugar (see method)*
2 tsp tartaric acid	*2 tsp tartaric acid*
2 tbsp premixed Bentonite Suspension	*2 tbsp premixed Bentonite Suspension*

1 tsp pectic enzyme
1 tsp yeast nutrient (Gervin)
white wine yeast (Gervin)
water to 1 gallon (4.5 litres)

1 tsp pectic enzyme
1 tsp yeast nutrient (Gervin)
white wine yeast (Gervin)
water to 1 gallon

*The use of frozen fruit seems to give a better flavour and assists the breakdown of the fruit. It is more manageable as well.

Allow the fruit to defrost and then crush it. While waiting for it to defrost (about one day), make up a yeast starter.

Using the grape concentrate and sugar, make up the must to a total volume of about 1 gallon (5 litres) with an initial specific gravity of 1.075. The Bentonite (which is added at the start to assist in clearing) is well mixed in and all the other ingredients are added. Use a 2-gallon (9-litre) bucket with a close-fitting lid.

Allow the must to ferment for four days, keeping it well covered and stirring twice daily. It can then be strained through a fine nylon sieve, without being pressed hard, and placed in a demijohn with cork bung and air-lock. At a temperature of 21°C (70°F), the wine which achieved the award mentioned above fermented out in four weeks to an s.g. of 0.993 and cleared quickly. It was carefully racked into another gallon jar and topped up with cold water. Sorbate and sulphite were added as usual, and the wine was brilliantly clear in three weeks. It was racked again and bottled.

The wine was clear, stable and dry with a good bouquet, Chablis-style flavour and no residual sweetness. It was exhibited four months later.

Gooseberry Wine
(Medium)

MR LEN KERRIDGE OF NORTH ROMFORD WINE CIRCLE

THIRD PRIZE, ESSEX FEDERATION SHOW 1980

Imperial (Metric)
3 cans gooseberries
3 tbsp liquid malt extract
2 lb (900 g) sugar
2 tsp citric acid
3 tsp Tronozymol nutrient
2 tsp liquid tannin
*yeast (Vierka Steinberg, if
    possible)*
water to 1 gallon (4.5 litres)

American
3 cans gooseberries
3 tbsp liquid malt extract
1¾ lb sugar
2 tsp citric acid
3 tsp Tronozymol nutrient
2 tsp liquid tannin
*yeast (Vierka Steinberg, if
    possible)*
water to 1 gallon

Wash and then mash the gooseberries and place them in a fermentation bin or bucket. Dissolve the malt extract and sugar in warm water and add the solution to the fruit. Stir well and add the acid, tannin and nutrient. A half teaspoon of Bentonite may also be added at this stage. Make up to 1 gallon (4.5 litres) with water at 25°C (75°F) and add the yeast.

Ferment on the pulp for four days, then strain into a demijohn. Top up if necessary, fit an air-lock and ferment out to required degree of sweetness (hydrometer reading 1.000 for a medium wine or 1.010 to 1.020 for a sweet wine). Stabilize with sorbate and sulphite as normal, rack or filter as necessary.

Gooseberry and Apple Wine
(Dry)

MR NORMAN CHIVERTON OF WOOLSCOTT, WARWICKSHIRE

FIRST PRIZE, THE JUDGES' CLASS, THE NATIONAL SHOW 1983

Imperial (Metric)

2 lb (900 g) gooseberries (frozen)

3 lb (1.35 kg) Bramley apples

1 pint (550 ml) concentrated white grape juice (Solvino)

sugar (see method)

2 tsp tartaric acid

2 tbsp premixed Bentonite Suspension

1 tsp pectic enzyme

1 tsp yeast nutrient (Gervin)

white wine yeast (Gervin)

water to 1 gallon (4.5 litres)

American

1¾ lb gooseberries (frozen)

2½ lb Bramley apples

1 pint concentrated white grape juice (Solvino)

sugar (see method)

2 tsp tartaric acid

2 tbsp premixed Bentonite Suspension

1 tsp pectic enzyme

1 tsp yeast nutrient (Gervin)

white wine yeast (Gervin)

water to 1 gallon

The apples can be crushed in a crusher and the gooseberries mashed with a potato masher once they have been thawed. Add the grape concentrate and make the volume up to 5 litres with sugar dissolved in warm water. Aim for a specific gravity of 1.075 to start. Mix in the Bentonite, then add an active yeast starter and all the other ingredients. Cover well (use a 2-gallon bucket with a close-fitting lid) and ferment for four days, stirring twice daily.

After four days, strain the must through a fine nylon sieve without pressing hard, and transfer the liquid to a 1-gallon (4.5 litre) jar with an air-lock. At a temperature of 21°C (70°F), the wine which achieved the award mentioned above fermented out in three weeks to a specific gravity of 0.992 and cleared very quickly. The wine was racked carefully into another demijohn and topped up with cold water. One Campden tablet and potassium sorbate were added. The wine was brilliantly clear in two weeks; half was stored in a ½-gallon (2.3-litre) jar and the other half was drunk.

The wine proved to be clear, stable and pleasantly dry with a white Burgundy style. The bouquet developed nicely and there was no residual sweetness. Four months later, the wine was exhibited.

Gooseberry and Elderflower Wine
(Dry)

MR R. MARSH OF BRISTOL

FIRST PRIZE, DRY WHITE WINE CLASS,
WALES AND WEST OF ENGLAND FESTIVAL 1978

Imperial (Metric)
3 lb (1.35 kg) green
  gooseberries
1 pint (550 ml) concentrated
  white grape juice
½ pint (300 ml) elderflowers
1½ lb (700 g) sugar
pectic enzyme
yeast (Chablis) and nutrients
water to 1 gallon (4.5 litres)

American
2½ lb green gooseberries

1 pint concentrated white
  grape juice
½ pint elderflowers
1¼ lb sugar
pectic enzyme
yeast (Chablis) and nutrients
water to 1 gallon

The ingredients listed above were used to make 1 gallon (4.5 litres) of dry white wine; the fruit pulp was then used to make another gallon of wine which achieved First Prize at the Wales and West of England Festival. The method below explains how to make both batches of wine.

Wash the gooseberries and top and tail them. Put them in a bucket with the sugar and add 6 pints (3.5 litres) of boiling water. When cool, add the enzyme, nutrient and yeast starter. Ferment on the pulp for two days, crushing the fruit by hand each day. Keep covered.

Strain off the liquid into a 1-gallon (4.5-litre) demijohn and add the grape concentrate. Fit an air-lock and when the first vigorous fermentation has died away, top up with cool boiled water. Ferment to dryness and rack as necessary when the fermentation has finished (specific gravity around 0.990), using a quarter of a Campden tablet each time. Bottle when clear.

The pulp obtained when straining off the liquid contains enough yeast to carry out a second fermentation as described below.

Imperial (Metric)

gooseberry fruit pulp
1 pint (550 ml) concentrated grape juice
¼ pint (150 ml) elderflowers
1 can frozen orange juice (Birds Eye Florida)
1 lb (450 g) sugar
8 oz (225 g) clear honey
a tip of a teaspoonful of tannin
2 tsp nutrient
water to 1 gallon (4.5 litres)

American

gooseberry fruit pulp
1 pint concentrated grape juice
¼ pint elderflowers
1 can frozen orange juice (Birds Eye Florida)
12 oz sugar
8 oz clear honey
a tip of a teaspoonful of tannin
2 tsp nutrient
water to 1 gallon

Dissolve the sugar and honey in 5 pints (2.8 litres) of hot water. When the solution has cooled, add it to the fruit pulp together with the nutrient, elderflowers and tannin. Ferment on the pulp for three days, then strain off the pulp, pressing lightly. Add the grape concentrate and the frozen orange juice and adjust the volume to about 6 pints (3.5 litres) in the demijohn. Top up with cool, boiled water when the fermentation abates. Rack early, and then as necessary, using a quarter of a Campden tablet each time. Bottle when clear and dry.

Grape Wine
(Rosé)

MR DON WAKELING OF TOTTERIDGE, LONDON

FIRST PRIZE (ROSÉ), HERTFORD FESTIVAL 1984

Imperial (Metric)	**American**
40 lb (18 kg) fresh red grapes★	32 lb fresh red grapes★
6¾ lb (3 kg) sugar (approx.)	5½ lb sugar (approx.)
1 Vitamin B tablet	1 Vitamin B tablet
Pectolase	Pectolase
Rohament P	Rohament P
3 tsp nutrient	3 tsp nutrient
yeast (Gervin Number 1)	yeast (Gervin Number 1)
water is not required	water is not required

★The quantities can be adjusted, depending on the grapes you have available. Work on the assumption that 12 lb (5.5 kg) of grapes will produce about 1 gallon (4.5 litres) of wine.

English red grapes can be disappointing in flavour and colour, and, if fermented on the pulp, may produce a bitter wine. This method takes off the juice fairly quickly yet gives a pleasant rosé colour. It is based on cold-greenhouse grown fruit.

Remove the grapes from their stems and cover with boiling water. When cool, crush the grapes (being careful not to break the pips) and add Rohament P and Pectolase according to manufacturer's instruction. Leave for four to five days keeping covered but crushing grapes daily. Then strain off the juice onto all the other ingredients and add the sugar, which should be adjusted to specific gravity 1.080; the quantity needed will depend on the ripeness of the grapes. Transfer to fermentation vessel under air-lock and proceed as normal.

Grapefruit Aperitif

FIRST PRIZE, NORTH-WEST FEDERATION SHOW 1983

Imperial (Metric)
10 ripe grapefruit
½ pint (300 ml) concentrated
  white grape juice
8 oz (225 g) sultanas
2¼ lb (1 kg) sugar
1 tsp Pectolase
1 tsp yeast nutrient
1 Vitamin B¹ tablet
yeast (as starter)
water to 1 gallon (4.5 litres)

American
10 ripe grapefruit
½ pint concentrated white
  grape juice
8 oz sultanas
1¾ lb sugar
1 tsp Pectolase
1 tsp yeast nutrient
1 Vitamin B¹ tablet
yeast (as starter)
water to 1 gallon

Peel the grapefruit and remove as much pith as possible from the flesh. Crush the fruit and place it in a pan or basin with the chopped sultanas. Pour 2 pints (1.2 litres) of boiling water over the fruit and stir well. Then strain the liquid onto the sugar in a fermentation bin or bucket. Repeat this process twice more with the pulp and then discard it.

Stir the sugar until it is completely dissolved, then allow the solution to cool before adding the Pectolase, nutrient and yeast. Cover and leave to ferment for three or four days, stirring daily. Then pour the liquid on to the grape concentrate in a demijohn and mix well. Fit an air-lock and leave the wine to ferment. Extra sugar may be added sparingly to increase the strength [say 2 oz (60 g) every time the specific gravity falls to 1.000 — Ed] but try to finish the wine dry. If you prefer a sweet aperitif, the adjustment can easily be made when the wine is clear and stable.

Grapefruit and Orange Aperitif

MR T. CORDWELL OF DERBY

WINE OF THE SHOW, LONG EATON OPEN FESTIVAL 1983

Imperial (Metric)	**American**
For 2 gallons (9 litres):	
7 fresh grapefruit	*7 fresh grapefruit*
9 fresh large oranges	*9 fresh large oranges*
1 lb (450 g) sultanas	*12 oz sultanas*
1 lb (450 g) apples	*1 lb apples*
8 oz (225 g) bananas	*8 oz bananas*
5 lb (2.3 kg) sugar (approx.)	*4 lb sugar (approx.)*
2 tsp grape tannin	*2 tsp grape tannin*
2 Vitamin B tablets	*2 Vitamin B tablets*
2 tsp pectic enzyme	*2 tsp pectic enzyme*
2 tsp yeast nutrient	*2 tsp yeast nutrient*
yeast (Madeira)	*yeast (Madeira)*
water to 2 gallons (9 litres)	*water to 2 gallons*

Thinly peel one grapefruit and one orange with a potato peeler. Place the rind, excluding any pith, in a fermentation bucket. Put the flesh of all the fruit except the bananas into a liquidizer with a little boiled water and thoroughly liquidize. Remove the pips and place the pulp in the bucket. Simmer the peeled, chopped bananas in sufficient water for five minutes, then strain the resulting "juice" into the bucket. Make up the volume to just under 2 gallons (9 litres) with boiling water in which 4¼ lb (1.9 kg) of sugar has been dissolved. Add the grape tannin and allow to cool overnight.

Next day, add the nutrients, pectic enzyme and an active yeast starter. Leave to ferment on the pulp for two days, keeping covered and stirring occasionally.

Strain the must through a nylon bag to remove the pulp, and return the liquid to the bucket. Leave for another twenty-four hours, keeping the bucket covered, then transfer the wine equally to two clean demijohns. Dissolve 6 oz (160 g) of sugar in each demijohn and mix well.

Continue feeding sugar in small amounts (2 oz; 55 g) each time the s.g. drops below 1.010 until the fermentation finally ceases. Rack the wine off the sediment into two clean demijohns and move them to a cool place. Rack again in the normal way as required until the wine is fully clear.

Sweeten with sugar to taste (the batch in question was sweetened to s.g. 1.035). Three teaspoonfuls of T. Noirot Vermouth Essence may be added per gallon (4.5 litres); the wine should be matured for at least one year.

Greengage and Gooseberry Wine
(Dry Table Wine)

HIGHLY COMMENDED, NORTH-WEST FEDERATION SHOW

Imperial (Metric)	American
3 lb (1.35 kg) bottled greengages	2½ lb bottled greengages
3 lb (1.35 kg) bottled gooseberries	2½ lb bottled gooseberries
¼ pint (150 ml) concentrated white grape juice	¼ pint concentrated white grape juice
1 lb (450 g) golden syrup	1 lb golden syrup
sugar (see method)	sugar (see method)
½ tsp malic acid	½ tsp malic acid
pectic enzyme	pectic enzyme

yeast and nutrient
water to 1 gallon (4.5 litres)

yeast and nutrient
water to 1 gallon

Although this recipe seems rather "heavy" on fruit, the finished wine is well worth it and in fact the bottled fruit is surprisingly cheap, particularly the imported variety by "Fruta".

Pour the grape concentrate, greengages, gooseberries and the syrup in which they are bottled into a sterilized fermentation bucket. Next, dissolve the golden syrup in about 2 pints (1.2 litres) of hot or boiling water, allow the solution to cool, and then add it to the bucket. Make the volume up to just under the gallon (4.5 litres) and if you have a hydrometer take a specific gravity reading. Calculate the amount of sugar necessary for an initial s.g. of about 1.080 and then dissolve this in the wine. If you don't have a hydrometer, then simply add about 8 oz (225 g) of granulated sugar, preferably dissolving it in a little water first. The hydrometer is useful because the amount of sugar in the bottled fruit does seem to vary somewhat.

Mash the fruit gently with a spoon, or crush it with your hands wearing sterilized rubber gloves. Take care not to break any of the stones or the wine will be ruined with an irreversible almond flavour. Add all the other ingredients, stir, cover and leave to ferment on the pulp for four days, stirring twice daily.

Then strain carefully into a demijohn and top up with water to the base of the neck. Fit an air-lock and ferment to completion. Leave for two or three days to settle, then rack and add 1 Campden tablet. Top up with water and leave to clear, then rack again. The wine should be dry with a fruity flavour and will be ready between three and six months after the final racking. Allow the wine at least one month in bottle before drinking it.

Mead
(Dry or Sweet)

MR TREVOR CHARLICK OF HUTTON WINE CIRCLE

FIRST PRIZE FOR BOTH DRY AND SWEET MEAD CLASSES,
ESSEX FEDERATION SHOWS 1982–1984

Imperial (Metric)
For 2 gallons (9 litres):
8½ lb (4 kg) Crete honey★
3½ pints (2 litres)
  unsweetened apple juice
juice of 2 lemons
½ tsp tartaric acid
1 tsp malic acid
1 tsp grape tannin
1 oz (30 g) yeast nutrient
2 Vitamin B tablets
2 tsp Pectolase
Tokay yeast (or other high-
  alcohol-tolerance)
water to 2 gallons (9 litres)

American
7 lb Crete honey★
3½ pints unsweetened apple
  juice
juice of 2 lemons
½ tsp tartaric acid
1 tsp malic acid
1 tsp grape tannin
1 oz yeast nutrient
2 Vitamin B tablets
2 tsp Pectolase
Tokay yeast (or other high-
  alcohol-tolerance)
water to 2 gallons

★Almost any mild honey can be used to make mead — clover honey is a common favourite. However, do avoid Australian honey, which can impart a pronounced eucalyptus flavour to the finished mead. Other flavourings you can use instead of apple juice include rosehip syrup, lemon and orange, and blackcurrant syrup — Ed.

Bring the honey to the boil in 3 pints (1.7 litres) of water and simmer for fifteen minutes. Skim off any scum that may develop. Remove from heat and allow to cool before adding the apple juice and the rest of the ingredients. Divide the liquid into two parts and put each in a demijohn, then top up with cool, boiled water until the specific gravity is about 1.120. Fit air-locks and leave to ferment. For a sweet mead, ferment until the s.g. reaches 1.020, then rack off the sediment and add a Campden tablet to each jar. For a dry mead, ferment the mead right out, then rack and add a Campden tablet. When clear, bottle and store for six months before use.

Mead
(Sweet)

MRS MARIE D'ARCY OF CHIGWELL WINE CIRCLE

FIRST PRIZE, SWEET MEAD CLASS, ESSEX WINEMAKERS' FEDERATION SHOW 1985

Imperial (Metric)
3–4 lb (1.35–1.8 kg) clover honey
3 tsp acid blend
½ tsp tannic acid
¼ tsp Epsom salts
2 tsp yeast nutrient
3 Vitamin B¹ tablets
yeast (Madeira) and nutrient
water to 1 gallon (4.5 litres)

American
3 lb clover honey

3 tsp acid blend
½ tsp tannic acid
¼ tsp Epsom salts
2 tsp yeast nutrient
3 Vitamin B¹ tablets
yeast (Madeira) and nutrient
water to 1 gallon

For a successful mead, use a single honey. This recipe specifies clover since this is a little more full-bodied for a sweet mead.

Dissolve 3 lb (1.35 kg) of the honey with warm water and pour into a sterilized demijohn together with the additives and 2 Campden tablets. Make the volume up to just under the gallon (4.5 litres) with cool, boiled water and leave to stand for twenty-four hours before adding the yeast starter.

Fit an air-lock and leave to ferment until the specific gravity falls to 1.010, then add 4 oz (110 g) of honey [dissolving this in a little boiling water will make the addition easier and ensure the honey is sterile — Ed.] Repeat this process each time the specific gravity falls to 1.010 until the fermentation finally finishes at 1.030. Add 2 Campden tablets and rack after one week. Continue to rack the mead every three months until the wine is clear, topping up as necessary. This mead should be kept for at least three years, but is well worth waiting for; it won this prize when seven years old.

Mixed Fruit Wine
(Dry Red Wine)

MR ROY SMALES OF NOTTINGHAM

BEST FRUIT WINE, THE NATIONAL SHOW 1978

Imperial (Metric)
5 lb (2.3 kg) blackberries
1½ lb (700 g) elderberries
2 lb (900 g) red grapes
3 lb (1.35 kg) sugar
2 tsp pectic enzyme
2 tsp yeast nutrient
yeast (Port type)
water to 1 gallon (4.5 litres)

American
4 lb blackberries
1¼ lb elderberries
1¾ lb red grapes
2½ lb sugar
2 tsp pectic enzyme
2 tsp yeast nutrient
yeast (Port type)
water to 1 gallon

For this method, you will need a strong plastic bag which is used inside a bucket to support it. The fruit is picked around the first week of September and is used immediately.

Boil the blackberries and elderberries in 6 pints (3.5 litres) of water for one minute. Add 2 lb (900 g) of sugar and stir to dissolve. Allow to cool, then add the pectic enzyme and nutrient and pour the mixture into the plastic bag.

Add the grapes, after first mashing them, and the yeast. Tie up the plastic bag firmly at the neck with an elastic band.

After one week, add another 8 oz (225 g) of sugar and stir until dissolved. Tie up the plastic bag. After a further week, strain the liquid out of the plastic bag into a demijohn and make up to 1 gallon (4.5 litres) with cool, boiled water in which 8 oz (225 g) of sugar has been dissolved. Fit an air-lock.

After two or three weeks the wine should have stopped fermenting and it should then be siphoned carefully into another demijohn, leaving behind all the sediment. Dissolve 1 crushed Campden tablet in the wine and add a wine-fining agent such as "Winecleer".

When the wine is clear, it is ready for bottling but will need two years to mature to bring out the fruitiness. The wine should have used up all the sugar and be dry with an alcohol content of about 16%; it can therefore be stored quite safely without any danger of it starting to re-ferment. When you wish to drink it, if you prefer a sweet wine, just add sugar to the bottle to taste. The plastic-bag method seems to allow the wine to breath and the finished wine appears to have a much fruitier blackberry characteristic.

Mixed Fruit Wine
(Medium Dry Red Wine)

MR H. APPLEBY OF SALE, CHESHIRE

FIRST PRIZE, NORTH-WEST FEDERATION SHOW 1980

Imperial (Metric)
1 lb (450 g) morello cherries bottled in syrup
1½ lb (700 g) raspberries (fresh or frozen)
1 × A1 can blackberries
3 oz (90 g) dried elderberries
1 can (1 kg) concentrated red grape juice (Solvino)
1 tsp Pectolase

American
1 lb morello cherries bottled in syrup
1¼ lb raspberries (fresh or frozen)
1 can blackberries
3 oz dried elderberries
1 pint concentrated red grape juice (Solvino)
1 tsp Pectolase

1 tsp Rohament P	1 tsp Rohament P
1 Vitamin B tablet	1 Vitamin B tablet
yeast (Burgundy) and nutrient	yeast (Burgundy) and nutrient
water to 1 gallon (4.5 litres)	water to 1 gallon

This recipe should achieve an initial s.g. of 1.080 without added sugar. Wash the elderberries, cover them with boiling water and leave to stand overnight. Then add the cherries, raspberries and blackberries, together with the Rohament P, 1 tsp of Bentonite and 1 crushed Campden tablet. Cover and leave for twenty-four hours, then add half of the concentrate with the nutrients and Vitamin B. Stir in the yeast and Pectolase, cover loosely and ferment for four days, stirring daily.

Strain into a demijohn and add the remaining concentrate. Fill up to the shoulder with cold boiled water, fit an air-lock and allow to ferment until the specific gravity reaches 1.000 or 1.002. Stabilize with a Campden tablet and sorbate as usual, and rack into a clean demijohn. Repeat the racking after three months, and bottle the wine when it is perfectly clear. Keep for one year before use.

A useful tip is to add 1 pint (600 ml) of cool, boiled water to the bucket after straining off the must. This is left for twenty-four hours, then strained into a litre bottle and plugged with cotton wool. After the first racking this can be used to top up the demijohn.

Mixed Fruit Wine
(Red Social Wine)

MR DAVID SIMMS OF BRACKLEY AND DISTRICT WINE CLUB

SECOND PRIZE, WALES AND WEST OF ENGLAND FEDERATION
SHOW 1984

Imperial (Metric)

For 2 gallons (9 litres):
3 lb (1.35 kg) blackberries
3 lb (1.35 kg) elderberries
3 lb (1.35 kg) sloes
3 lb (1.35 kg) damsons
14 oz (450 g) strawberries
   (canned)
14 oz (450 g) cherries
   (canned)
14 oz (450 g) raspberries
   (canned)
2 × 8 oz cans (450 g)
   concentrated red grape juice
5 lb (2.3 kg) sugar
1 tsp citric acid
pectic enzyme
Vitamin B¹ tablet
yeast (Bordeaux) and nutrient
water to 2 gallons (9 litres)

American

2½ lb blackberries
2½ lb elderberries
2½ lb sloes
2½ lb damsons
12 oz strawberries (canned)

12 oz cherries (canned)

12 oz raspberries (canned)

12 oz concentrated red grape
   juice
4 lb sugar
1 tsp citric acid
pectic enzyme
Vitamin B¹ tablet
yeast (Bordeaux) and nutrient
water to 2 gallons

Wash all the fresh fruit and place it in a bucket with the canned fruit. Add 6 pints (3.5 litres) of boiling water and all the other ingredients except the yeast. Then make up to 14 pints (8.5 litres) with cold water. Ensure the sugar is thoroughly dissolved, then add the yeast and stir well. Leave to ferment on the pulp for four days, keeping well covered and stirring twice daily. Strain into two 1-gallon (4.5-litres) jars, top up, fit air-locks and ferment out. Rack and stabilize the wine, leave it to clear and rack again if necessary. Bottle the wine, sweetening as necessary before use.

Mixed Fruit Red Dessert Wine

MR DON SAYERS OF PEASMARSH, EAST SUSSEX

Imperial (Metric)
For 2 gallons (9 litres):
1½ lb (700 g) dried apricots★
4 oz (110 g) dried elderberries
1 lb (450 g) bottled bilberries in syrup
8 oz (225 g) raisins (chopped)
4 oz (110 g) prunes (soft variety)
2½ lb (1.15 kg) sugar
1 Vitamin B¹ tablet
2 tsp Pectolase
yeast and nutrient
water to 2 gallons (9 litres)

American
1¼ lb dried apricots★
4 oz dried elderberries
1 lb bottled bilberries in syrup
8 oz raisins (chopped)
4 oz prunes (soft variety)
2 lb sugar
1 Vitamin B¹ tablet
2 tsp Pectolase
yeast and nutrient
water to 2 gallons

★The lighter the dried apricots' colour, the more sulphite they contain as a preservative. This could hinder the fermentation, so try to find the darker coloured ones, and chop them before use.

Put the fruit into a suitable container and pour on about 2 gallons (9 litres) of boiling water in which 8 oz (225 g) of sugar has been dissolved. When the liquid has cooled to 20°C (70°F), add the nutrients, Pectolase and yeast. Cover and ferment at 20–25°C (68–75°F) for three days, stirring daily. (A 20 mg Vitamin C tablet can also be added at this stage as a precaution against oxidation.)

After three days, strain through a coarse and then a fine straining mesh and put the liquid in a bucket. Add the rest of the sugar and stir to dissolve, then split the wine equally between two demijohns and fit air-locks. Keep checking the specific gravity, and when it has fallen to about 1.020 start "feeding" with sugar. Dissolve and thoroughly mix 4 oz (110 g) of sugar into the wine each time the s.g. falls below 1.020 and repeat the process until the fermentation finally stops. Finish the wine strong and sweet, aiming for a final s.g. of about 1.025. Rack off the sediment and dissolve 3 Campden tablets in the wine. Store for about a year. When bottling, add 3–4 drops of almond essence per bottle if you wish.

Mixed Fruit Wine

(Red Dessert Wine)

MR T. CORDWELL OF DERBY

SECOND PRIZE, EAST MIDLANDS FEDERATION SHOW 1980

Imperial (Metric)	**American**
For 2 gallons (9 litres):	
1 can (1 kg) bilberry and grape concentrate (CWE)★	1 pint bilberry and grape concentrate (CWE)★
2 lb (900 g) blackberries (frozen)	1¾ lb blackberries (frozen)
2 lb (900 g) black grapes (frozen)	1¾ lb black grapes (frozen)
2 lb (900 g) elderberries (frozen)	1¾ lb elderberries (frozen)
1 lb (450 g) bananas	12 oz bananas
up to 4 lb (1.8 kg) sugar (see method)	3½ lb sugar (see method)
2 tsp pectic enzyme	2 tsp pectic enzyme
2 Vitamin B tablets	2 Vitamin B tablets

yeast *(Madeira type if*
   possible) and nutrient
water to 2 gallons (9 litres)

yeast *(Madeira type if*
   possible) and nutrient
water to 2 gallons

*If this is not available when you make the wine, use an ordinary can of concentrated grape juice and a jar of bottled bilberries. Alternatively, you could try using a can of blackcurrants — Ed.

Prepare a yeast starter. Put the frozen fruit into a bucket with 1 gallon (4.5 litres) of boiling water. When cool, dissolve 2 Campden tablets in the liquid to sterilize the fruit and leave overnight.

Next day, peel and chop the bananas, simmer the flesh for fifteen minutes in water, then strain the resulting liquor into the bucket. Macerate the fruit using a hand-held liquidizer or a spoon and add the grape concentrate, pectic enzyme, nutrient and the yeast starter. Leave to ferment for five days, keeping well covered and stirring frequently. (If a cap of seeds rises to the surface it may be skimmed off and discarded.)

On the seventh day, strain the liquid into a clean bucket and make the volume up to slightly less than 2 gallons (9 litres) with cool, boiled water in which 1¼ lb (500 g) of sugar has been dissolved. This will ensure there is room for the sugar which has yet to be added.

Next day, dissolve another 1¼ lb (500 g) of sugar in the must. Leave the must in the bucket to ferment for a further two days before dividing it between two clean demijohns. Dissolve 4 oz (110 g) of sugar in each demijohn. Fit air-locks.

When the specific gravity has fallen to about 1.012, dissolve a further 5 oz (130 g) of sugar in each jar. Repeat this process, feeding the sugar in small doses, until the fermentation finally ends.

Rack the wine into clean demijohns and move them to a cool place. Repeat the racking as necessary until the wine is completely clear. The batch which achieved the award mentioned above was sweetened to an s.g. of 1.040 with sugar, and 3 dessertspoons of glycerine were added per gallon (4.5 litres). The wine was then matured for one year.

Mixed Fresh Fruit Rosé
(Medium Dry)

MRS F. HAWKIN OF HELSBY, CHESHIRE

MID-CHESHIRE SHOW PRIZEWINNER

Imperial (Metric)
2¼ lb (1 kg) redcurrants
6 oz (170 g) mixed
   raspberries and
   loganberries
6 oz (170 g) strawberries
2 lb (900 g) sugar
¾ tsp acid blend (citric,
   tartaric, malic)
¼ tsp tannin
pectic enzyme
nutrient
yeast (preferably Gervin
   Number 1)
water to 1 gallon (4.5 litres)

American
1¾ lb redcurrants
6 oz mixed raspberries and
   loganberries

6 oz strawberries
1¾ lb sugar
¾ tsp acid blend (citric,
   tartaric, malic)
¼ tsp tannin
pectic enzyme
nutrient
yeast (preferably Gervin
   Number 1)
water to 1 gallon

Put the sugar and the fruit into a sterilized bucket. Pour on boiling water to dissolve the sugar and stir well. Top up with cool, boiled water to 1 gallon (4.5 litres). When the must has reached fermentation temperature, add the acids, tannin, nutrient, pectic enzyme and yeast. Leave covered for two to three days, stirring daily, and then strain into a demijohn, fit an air-lock and ferment to dryness.

Rack, sulphite and top up the wine as normal; rose petal wine is useful for topping up as this can enhance the bouquet.

(Another useful idea is to make a wine from grape concentrate and use this for topping up.) The wine should be sweetened slightly (dry to medium) and is best served chilled.

Mixed Fruit White Table Wine

FYLDE AMATEUR WINEMAKERS' GUILD
THIRD PRIZE, NORTH-WEST FEDERATION SHOW 1981

Imperial (Metric)

15 oz (450 g) canned peaches
8 oz (225 g) canned gooseberries
½ pint (300 ml) apple juice
½ pint (300 ml) grapefruit juice
½ pint (300 ml) concentrated white grape juice
1½ lb (700 g) sugar
½ tsp tartaric acid
½ tsp malic acid
¼ tsp grape tannin
1 tsp Pectolase
1 tsp nutrient
yeast (general-purpose)
1 tsp dried elderflowers or dried rose petals
water to 1 gallon (4.5 litres)

American

15 oz canned peaches
8 oz canned gooseberries
½ pint apple juice
½ pint grapefruit juice
½ pint concentrated white grape juice
1¼ lb sugar
½ tsp tartaric acid
½ tsp malic acid
¼ tsp grape tannin
1 tsp Pectolase
1 tsp nutrient
yeast (general-purpose)
1 tsp dried elderflowers or dried rose petals
water to 1 gallon

Place the peaches and gooseberries in a plastic bin or bucket and mash the fruit. Pour on 2 pints (1.2 litres) of boiling water. Add the sugar, apple juice, grapefruit juice and grape concentrate, and stir until all the sugar has dissolved before making up to 1 gallon (4.5 litres) with cool, boiled water.

Then add the acids, tannin, pectic enzyme, yeast and nutrient. Cover with a cloth and leave to ferment in a warm place for six days, stirring daily. On the third day sprinkle in 1 tsp of dried elderflowers or ½ oz (15 g) of dried rose petals to enhance the bouquet. Strain through a nylon mesh bag into a 1-gallon (4.5-litre) jar. Top up with cool, boiled water if necessary, fit an air-lock and ferment out.

When the fermentation is complete, rack off the sediment and dissolve 1 Campden tablet and 1 sorbate tablet in the wine. One month later rack again, and filter the wine if necessary. Sweeten to taste with a little sugar syrup. Bottle and mature.

Nectarine and Apricot Dessert Wine

MR J. BANKS OF GREAT HARWOOD, LANCASHIRE

FIRST PRIZE, THE NATIONAL SHOW 1980

Imperial (Metric)
6 nectarines
8 oz (225 g) dried apricots
1 lb (450 g) greengages
8 oz (225 g) figs
3 bananas
1 tsp dried elderflowers
8 fl oz (250 ml) concentrated
   white grape juice
juice of 3 oranges
3 lb (1.35 kg) sugar
¼ tsp grape tannin
2 Vitamin B¹ tablets
1 tsp Pectolase
yeast (general-purpose) and
   nutrient)
water to 1 gallon (4.5 litres)

American
6 nectarines
8 oz dried apricots
12 oz greengages
6 oz figs
3 bananas
1 tsp dried elderflowers
⅓ pint concentrated white
   grape juice
juice of 3 oranges
2½ lb sugar
¼ tsp grape tannin
2 Vitamin B¹ tablets
1 tsp Pectolase
yeast (general-purpose) and
   nutrient
water to 1 gallon

Place the figs in a bucket, cover with 1 pint (600 ml) of boiling water and leave overnight. Next day, remove the stones from the nectarines and greengages, and put them in a pan with the apricots. Add 2 pints (1.2 litres) of water and bring to the boil. Simmer for fifteen minutes, then pour the fruit and liquid over the figs. Add 2 lb (900 g) of sugar and stir well to dissolve. Allow to cool, then add the peeled, chopped bananas, the juice of the oranges, the dried elderflowers, the pectic enzyme, tannin, nutrients and 4 pints (2.3 litres) of cold water. Check that the must is at the correct temperature then add the yeast and pulp ferment for seven days, keeping well covered and stirring daily.

After this period, pour the grape concentrate into a demijohn and add the liquid strained off the pulp. Fit an air-lock and ferment for five days. Next, rack off the sediment and dissolve 8 oz (225 g) of sugar in the wine. Refit an air-lock and ferment for a further five days before adding the final 8 oz (225 g) of sugar. Allow the fermentation to continue until the desired level of strength and sweetness is achieved. Stabilize, rack and bottle as normal.

Orange Juice Wine
(Medium Dry)

MRS DOT JONES OF HUYTON WINEMAKERS' GUILD

FIRST PRIZE, HUYTON WINEMAKERS' GUILD ANNUAL SHOW 1985

Imperial (Metric)
3½ pints (2 litres) pure
  orange juice (with no
  additives)
1 small can concentrated white
  grape juice
2½ lb (1.15 kg) sugar

American
3½ pints pure orange juice
  (with no additives)

1 small can concentrated white
  grape juice
2 lb sugar

3 Vitamin B¹ tablets
1 tsp Pectolase
1 tsp yeast nutrient
yeast (general-purpose)
water to 1 gallon (4.5 litres)

3 Vitamin B¹ tablets
1 tsp Pectolase
1 tsp yeast nutrient
yeast (general-purpose)
water to 1 gallon

Prepare a yeast starter bottle in the normal way and leave it for about five hours. Then pour the starter into a 1-gallon (4.5-litre) demijohn and add all the other ingredients. (It is best to dissolve the sugar in water before adding it to the demijohn.) Mix well, top up with cool, boiled water, fit an air-lock and ferment out. Rack and bottle in the usual way. This wine needs about twelve months to mature.

Orange Wine
(Medium Dry)

MRS J.C. PROVIS OF LEICESTER AMATEUR WINEMAKERS' CIRCLE

LOCAL CIRCLE PRIZEWINNING WINE

Imperial (Metric)
10 oranges
2 bananas
½ can (500 g) concentrated white grape juice (white medium dry)
2 lb 10 oz (1.2 kg) sugar
¼ tsp grape tannin
1 tsp pectic enzyme
yeast and nutrient
water to 1 gallon (4.5 litres)

American
10 oranges
2 bananas
½ pint concentrated white grape juice (white medium dry)
2 lb sugar
¼ tsp grape tannin
1 tsp pectic enzyme
yeast and nutrient
water to 1 gallon

Pare the rind from three of the oranges, taking care to avoid any pith, which will give the wine a bitter taste. Squeeze the juice from all the oranges and put it in a bucket with the rind. Dissolve 2 lb (900 g) of sugar in 2 pints (1.2 litres) of hot water and add this solution to the bucket together with a further 2 pints (1.2 litres) of boiling water. Allow to cool, then add pectic enzyme in accordance with the manufacturer's instructions. Cover and leave for twenty-four hours.

Next day, simmer the peeled, sliced bananas in ½ pint (300 ml) of water for twenty minutes, allow to cool, then strain the resulting "juice" into the fermentation bucket. Add an active yeast. Ferment in the bucket for five to seven days, then strain into a demijohn and add the rest of the sugar dissolved in 1 pint (550 ml) of water. Top up to 1 gallon (4.5 litres) if necessary, fit an air-lock, and ferment to completion. Rack the wine into a clean demijohn, adding 1 Campden tablet and potassium sorbate if wished. Leave undisturbed for six months, then rack again. The wine should be clear and medium sweet.

Orange Vermouth

MRS DOROTHY NAYLOR OF ROMILEY AMATEUR WINE SOCIETY

FIRST PRIZE, ROMILEY AMATEUR WINE SOCIETY SHOW

Imperial (Metric)
3½ pints (2 litres) Jaffa
    orange juice
1 small can concentrated white
    grape juice
2¼ lb (1 kg) sugar
zest of 2 oranges
1 vanilla pod
Vermouth herbs
Pectolase
1 Vitamin B tablet

American
3½ pints Jaffa orange juice

1 small can concentrated white
    grape juice
1¾ lb sugar
zest of 2 oranges
1 vanilla pod
Vermouth herbs
Pectolase
1 Vitamin B tablet

<table>
<tr><td>yeast and nutrient</td><td>yeast and nutrient</td></tr>
<tr><td>water to 1 gallon (4.5 litres)</td><td>water to 1 gallon</td></tr>
</table>

Prepare a yeast starter. When it is fermenting well, mix it with the fruit juice, sugar (as syrup), pectic enzyme and nutrient in a demijohn. Make the volume up to 1 gallon (4.5 litres) and ferment to dryness.

Stabilize and rack as normal, then add extra sugar to taste. The flavour is obtained by suspending the rest of oranges, vanilla pod and Vermouth herbs (available from winemaking shops) in a sterile muslin bag in the wine until the flavour is strong enough for your palate.

Orange and Grapefruit Aperitif
(Dry Vermouth)

MRS F. HAWKIN OF HELSBY, CHESHIRE

MID-CHESHIRE SHOW PRIZEWINNER

Imperial (Metric)	**American**
10 oranges	*10 oranges*
2 grapefruit	*2 grapefruit*
8 oz (225 g) sultanas	*8 oz sultanas*
or ½ pint (300 ml) concentrated white grape juice	*or ½ pint concentrated white grape juice*
3 bananas	*3 bananas*
up to 3 lb (1.35 kg) sugar	*up to 2½ lb sugar*
¼ tsp grape tannin	*¼ tsp grape tannin*
1 tsp Pectolase	*1 tsp Pectolase*
White Vermouth essence (or herbs)	*White Vermouth essence (or herbs)*
yeast nutrient	*yeast nutrient*

yeast (Gervin high-alcohol
   tolerance)
water to 1 gallon (4.5 litres)

yeast (Gervin high-alcohol
   tolerance)
water to 1 gallon

Wash the fruit. Using a potato peeler, thinly peel the rind from 2 oranges and 1 grapefruit. Put the peelings into a pan with the peeled, sliced bananas and boil for ten minutes. Wash and mince the sultanas and put them, together with 2 lb (900 g) of sugar, in a sterilized fermentation bucket. Pour on 4 pints (2.3 litres) of boiling water and stir to dissolve the sugar. Add the liquid strained from the bananas and the juice of all the citrus fruit. Make up to 1 gallon (4.5 litres) with cool, boiled water.

Check that the must is at fermentation temperature, and then add the Pectolase, nutrient, tannin and yeast according to the manufacturer's instructions. Cover and ferment for three days, stirring every day, then strain into a gallon jar (4.5 litres). This type of wine should be high in alcohol, so it will be necessary to "feed" the wine when the specific gravity has dropped to about 1.010 with 4 oz (110 g) of sugar dissolved in a little of the wine. After two such feedings, the specific gravity should be allowed to fall to 1.005 and the sugar added in 2 oz (60 g) lots for as long as the yeast will work. This should allow you to produce a dry wine.

When the fermentation has finally finished, rack the wine off the sediment and top up with cool, boiled water in which 1 Campden tablet has been dissolved. Rack once more when necessary, add sulphite and top up as previously. Before bottling, draw off one bottle full of wine and carefully add White Vermouth essence (or the strained extract of the herbs) to the remainder. Use the single bottle to adjust the flavour, if necessary.

Orange, Pineapple and Elderflower Wine

(Dry)

MR DAVID ROBERTS OF TIMPERLEY WINE CIRCLE

HIGHLY COMMENDED, DRY WHITE AND GOLDEN WINE CLASS,
NORTH-WEST FEDERATION SHOW 1985

Imperial (Metric)

For 2 gallons (9 litres):
1¾ pints (1 litre) pure orange juice (carton)
1¾ pints (1 litre) pure pineapple juice (carton)
1 can (1 kg) concentrated white grape juice
4 tsp lemon juice
8 tsp dried elderflowers
3 lb (1.35 kg) sugar
Pectolase
yeast (preferably Gervin Number 3)
water to 2 gallons (9 litres)

American

1¾ pints pure orange juice (carton)
1¾ pints pure pineapple juice (carton)
1 can concentrated white grape juice
4 tsp lemon juice
8 tsp dried elderflowers
2½ lb sugar
Pectolase
yeast (preferably Gervin Number 3)
water to 2 gallons

Dissolve the sugar in a fermentation bin or bucket with hot water. When cool, add the orange juice, pineapple juice, concentrated grape juice, lemon juice and Pectolase.

Divide the must equally between two demijohns, top up to two-thirds full with water and fit air-locks. Don't fill the jars completely for the first few days because the wine has a very vigorous fermentation to begin with. Add the yeast as instructed on the packet, and the elderflowers (4 tsp to each jar) once the fermentation has started.

Leave the wine at a steady room temperature to ferment

out; this should take about two weeks. For a dry wine the final specific gravity should be 0.095–1.000. When the fermentation has ended, rack the wine off the sediment and add Campden tablets and potassium sorbate as instructed on the packet. The wine can be fined or filtered if required. Otherwise it can be bottled and drunk almost at once, but it does improve with keeping.

Parsnip Wine
(Sweet)

MRS JENNY HAWDON OF BISHOP AUCKLAND WINE CIRCLE

FIRST PRIZE, SWEET WHITE OR GOLDEN WINE,
NORTH-WEST FEDERATION SHOW 1984

Imperial (Metric)	**American**
2 lb (900 g) parsnips	*2 lb parsnips*
1 lb (450 g) raisins	*12 oz raisins*
4 lb (1.8 kg) sugar	*3½ lb sugar*
2 oranges	*2 oranges*
2 lemons	*2 lemons*
yeast and nutrient	*yeast and nutrient*
10 pints (3.5 litres) water	*10 pints water*

Scrub and grate the parsnips, then put the pieces into a large pan with 6 pints (3.5 litres) of water. Bring to the boil and simmer for five minutes, skimming off any froth. Strain the liquid through a muslin or nylon strainer and discard the pulp. Add 2 lb (900 g) of sugar to the hot liquid and stir until it has dissolved. Chop the raisins, oranges and lemons into small pieces and add them to the parsnip liquid. Allow to cool, then add yeast and nutrient and ferment for ten days, keeping well covered and stirring daily.

After ten days, strain through muslin or nylon, and discard

the pulp. Put 2 lb (900 g) of sugar into a pan with 4 pints (2.3 litres) of water, then bring to the boil and simmer for two minutes. Allow to cool, then stir this into the wine. Pour the wine into a fermentation vessel and fit an air-lock. Ferment until the yeast stops working or the specific gravity falls to 1.020. Sweeten if necessary. Rack and stabilize in the normal way using a Campden tablet and potassium sorbate.

Peach Wine

MR HAROLD HALLWOOD OF WIDNES WINE CIRCLE

FIRST PRIZE, WIDNES OPEN SHOW 1976

Imperial (Metric)
4 lb (1.8 kg) fresh peaches
8 oz (225 g) raisins
8 oz (225 g) pale malt
sugar (see method)
¼ tsp grape tannin
1 tsp tartaric acid
¼ tsp yeast nutrient
yeast (Sauternes)
water to 1 gallon (4.5 litres)

American
3½ lb fresh peaches
8 oz raisins
8 oz pale malt
sugar (see method)
¼ tsp grape tannin
1 tsp tartaric acid
¼ tsp yeast nutrient
yeast (Sauternes)
water to 1 gallon

Make a yeast starter bottle before preparing the wine.

Stone the peaches, cut them up and place them in a plastic bucket with the pale malt, minced raisins, acid, nutrient and tannin. Pour on cold water to the half gallon (2.3 litre) level and add 1 Campden tablet. Cover and leave for twenty-four hours.

Next day, add the yeast starter, mix well, then cover and leave for five to six days, stirring daily. Strain the liquid into a 1-gallon (4.5-litre) demijohn and add 1 lb (450 g) of sugar dissolved in sufficient water to bring the volume up to about 7

Leave $\overline{\text{FRIDAY}}$ for
3-5 days

0006205

Royal National Institute for the Blind

RNIB
challenging blindness

With your money RNIB can help people with serious sight problems achieve their full p...

GRAND DRAW 1999

50p

1st prize: £1000 cash
2nd prize: £500 cash
3rd prize: £250 cash

Drawn: Tuesday 22nd June 1999

Promoter: Patrick Holmes, RNIB Wales & West Region, Church Square, Taunton, Somerset, TA1 1SA.
Registered charity number 226227.
Registered under Schedule 1A to the Lotteries and Amusements Act 1976, with the Gaming Board for Great Britain.

All winners will be notified in writing by 1st July 1999. For a list of winners please enclose S.A.E.

Cusworth & Daniels Ltd. (Printers), 327 Whitehall Road, Leeds LS12 6AQ.

pints (4.0 litres). Check the specific gravity as the fermentation proceeds, and for a dessert wine keep adding 4 oz (110 g) of sugar each time the s.g. falls below 1.010. [For a dry wine, add a total of 2 lb (900 g) of sugar and make the volume up to 1 gallon (4.5 litres) — Ed.]

When the fermentation has finally achieved the desired degree of strength and sweetness, rack the wine off the sediment, stabilize with sorbate and Campden tablets as instructed on the packet, and top up as required. (The wine was improved by adding six hop leaves for the first two weeks of fermentation in the demijohn, after which they were strained out.) This turned out to be a good full-bodied dessert wine.

Peach, Apricot and Lychee Wine
(Sweet Social Wine)

MRS MARY GARSIDE OF HUDDERSFIELD, YORKSHIRE

FIRST PRIZE, NORTH-WEST FEDERATION SHOW 1984

Imperial (Metric)

For 2 gallons (9 litres):
29 oz (850 g) canned peaches
29 oz (850 g) canned apricots
29 oz (850 g) canned lychees
3 lb (1.35 kg) bananas
2¼ lb (1 kg) sultanas
4½ lb (2 kg) sugar (approx.)
4 oranges
2 lemons
1 tsp tartaric acid
1 tsp malic acid
1 tsp grape tannin
2 tsp Pectolase
1 tsp Tronozymol nutrient

American

1½ lb canned peaches
1½ lb canned apricots
1½ lb canned lychees
2½ lb bananas
1¾ lb sultanas
3¾ lb sugar (approx.)
4 oranges
2 lemons
1 tsp tartaric acid
1 tsp malic acid
1 tsp grape tannin
2 tsp Pectolase
1 tsp Tronozymol nutrient

yeast and nutrient
water to 2 gallons (9 litres)

yeast and nutrient
water to 2 gallons

Peel and chop the bananas and boil the pieces, together with half the skins, for thirty minutes in 3 pints (1.7 litres) of water. Strain the hot liquid on to the pulped tinned fruit and sultanas in a fermentation bucket. Add 2¼·lb (1 kg) of granulated sugar dissolved in water, the orange and lemon rind thinly pared to avoid any white pith, and the juice of the oranges and lemons. Make the volume up to just under 2 gallons (9 litres) and stir in the acids, Pectolase and nutrient. Check that the temperature is correct (20–25°C/70–75°F) before adding the yeast. Cover and ferment on the pulp for four days, stirring daily.

Strain into two demijohns, dissolving 8 oz (225 g) of sugar and 1 fl oz (30 ml) of glycerine in each one. Fit air-locks and ferment until the specific gravity falls below 1.010, then add 4 oz (110 g) of sugar to each jar; repeat the process as often as possible until the desired degree of strength and sweetness is achieved or the fermentation stops. Rack and stabilize in the normal way; if necessary sweeten the wine to a specific gravity of 1.020.

Peach and Elderflower Wine
(Social Wine)

MRS DOT JONES OF HUYTON WINEMAKERS' GUILD

SECOND PRIZE, WHITE COUNTRY AND SOCIAL WINE CLASS, HUYTON WINEMAKERS' GUILD ANNUAL SHOW 1984

Imperial (Metric)
2 lb (900 g) dried peaches
1 small can concentrated white grape juice

American
1¾ lb dried peaches
1 small can concentrated white grape juice

2 oz (60 g) dried elderflowers
2½ lb (1.15 kg) sugar
½ tsp malic acid
½ tsp citric acid
¼ tsp grape tannin
3 Vitamin B¹ tablets
1 tsp Pectolase
yeast and nutrient
water to 1 gallon (4.5 litres)

1½ oz dried elderflowers
2 lb sugar
½ tsp malic acid
½ tsp citric acid
¼ tsp grape tannin
3 Vitamin B¹ tablets
1 tsp Pectolase
yeast and nutrient
water to 1 gallon

Soak the dried peaches overnight in 6 pints (3.5 litres) of cold water. While the peaches are soaking, prepare a yeast starter bottle.

Next day, bring the peaches to the boil and simmer gently for ten minutes. Pour the peaches and boiling water over the sugar in a fermentation bin or bucket and stir to dissolve. Then add the dried elderflowers and stir again. Cover and allow to cool.

Add the yeast starter and all the other ingredients, cover and leave to ferment on the pulp for four days, stirring daily. Strain into a gallon jar (4.5 litres), top up with cool, boiled water, fit an air-lock and ferment out. Rack and top up as necessary. Keep for a year before drinking.

Pineapple and Lychee Wine
(Social Wine)

MR GEORGE SIMMONS OF TUDELEY, KENT

Imperial (Metric)
15 oz (425 g) canned lychees
1¾ pints (1 litre) pineapple
  juice

American
12 oz canned lychees
1¾ pints pineapple juice

½ pint (300 ml) concentrated
 white grape juice
2½ lb (1.15 kg) sugar
3 ripe bananas
½ tsp grape tannin
½ tsp citric acid
1 tsp pectic enzyme
½ tsp yeast nutrient
yeast
water to 1 gallon (4.5 litres)

½ pint concentrated white
 grape juice
2 lb sugar
3 ripe bananas
½ tsp grape tannin
½ tsp citric acid
1 tsp pectic enzyme
½ tsp yeast nutrient
yeast
water to 1 gallon

Boil the peeled, chopped bananas in 1 pint (550 ml) of water for ten minutes and then strain the resulting "juice" into a 1-gallon (4.5-litre) demijohn. Add the juice of the canned lychees — the fruit can be used in a fruit salad — and the pineapple juice. Dissolve 2 lb (900 g) of the sugar in 1 pint (550 ml) of hot water and add this to the demijohn. Allow to cool to fermentation temperature before adding the pectic enzyme, nutrient, tannin, citric acid and Bentonite. Top up with water to the shoulder of the jar and add the yeast. Fit an air-lock and leave to ferment, adding the remaining sugar in three equal amounts each time the s.g. falls to 1.020.

Finally, when the s.g. falls to 1.010, rack the wine off the sediment into a clean demijohn and add 2 Campden tablets and the recommended amount of potassium sorbate as a stabilizer to prevent further fermentation. Rack after three weeks, topping up as necessary with cool, boiled water. The wine is ready to drink at six months but better at twelve.

Plum Rosé
(Medium Dry)

MR H. APPLEBY OF SALE, CHESHIRE

SECOND PRIZE, NORTH-WEST FEDERATION SHOW 1981

Imperial (Metric)
4 lb (1.8 kg) ripe red plums
½ can (500 g) concentrated
  white grape juice
1½ lb (700 g) sugar
1 tsp tartaric acid
2 Vitamin B¹ tablets
2 tsp Pectolase
2 tsp yeast nutrient
yeast
water to 1 gallon (4.5 litres)

American
3½ lb ripe red plums
½ pint concentrated white
  grape juice
1¼ lb sugar
1 tsp tartaric acid
2 Vitamin B¹ tablets
2 tsp Pectolase
2 tsp yeast nutrient
yeast
water to 1 gallon

Wash the fruit thoroughly in very hot water to remove any waxy deposit on the skins. Remove the stones, chop the plums and place them in a fermentation bin or bucket. Cover with water containing 1 dissolved Campden tablet and leave for twenty-four hours with a cover over the bucket.

Dissolve the sugar in hot water and add the resulting solution to the fruit in the bucket. Top up to just under the gallon (4.5 litres) with cold, boiled water, leaving room for the grape concentrate. Check the must is at fermentation temperature, then add the nutrients, acid, pectic enzyme and yeast. Cover loosely and ferment on the pulp until a bright red colour has been achieved (about four days). Then strain into a demijohn, add the concentrated grape juice and top up if necessary with cold, boiled water. Fit an air-lock and ferment until the specific gravity falls to 1.000 or 1.002. Stabilize using a Campden tablet and potassium sorbate as usual. Rack as necessary, and bottle when the wine is perfectly clear. Keep for twelve months before use. The colour may fade slightly, but the wine should be a good, fruity, medium dry rosé.

Plum Wine
(Medium Golden Wine)

MRS JEAN PRICE OF CHORLEY WINE CIRCLE

FIRST PRIZE, WHITE OR GOLDEN WINE (MEDIUM) CLASS,
ACCRINGTON OPEN COMPETITION

Imperial (Metric)
2½ lb (1.15 kg) canned plums
8 oz (225 g) raisins
2½ lb (1.15 kg) sugar
¼ tsp tartaric acid
2 tsp nutrient
pectic enzyme
yeast
water to 1 gallon (4.5 litres)

American
2 lb canned plums
8 oz raisins
2 lb sugar
¼ tsp tartaric acid
2 tsp nutrient
pectic enzyme
yeast
water to 1 gallon

Open the cans, pour off and save the syrup. Mash the fruit and remove the stones, then place the fruit pulp in a bucket with the chopped raisins. Pour on 5 pints (2.8 litres) of boiling water. Cover and leave to cool, then stir in the pectic enzyme and leave for twenty-four hours.

Pour in the syrup from the canned fruit, and add the acid, nutrient and 1½ lb (700 g) of sugar dissolved in a little water. Mix well and at the correct fermentation temperature add the yeast. Cover and leave to ferment on the pulp for four days, stirring twice daily.

Strain into a demijohn and top up with water to bring up the volume to just under the gallon (4.5 litres). Allow to ferment for two to three weeks, then "feed" the remaining sugar in 4 oz (110 g) lots each time the s.g. falls to 1.005. When the fermentation has finally finished, rack off the sediment and add 1 Campden tablet and 1 sorbate tablet if desired. Rack again when the wine is perfectly clear, then mature as appropriate.

"Port"

MR E.K. MITCHELL OF ROMILEY WINEMAKERS

FOURTH PRIZE, RED DESSERT WINE CLASS,
NORTH-WEST FEDERATION SHOW 1985

[Those winemakers who like to ferment in bulk and mature in casks may like to try this recipe for "Port" by Mr Mitchell. Of course the quantities could be scaled down to make 1 gallon (4.5 litres) — Ed.]

Imperial (Metric)
For 6 gallons (27 litres):
40 lb (18 kg) elderberries
40 lb (18 kg) fresh black
   Hamburg grapes
10 lb (4.5 kg) bananas
2 lb (900 g) morello cherries
1 lb (450 g) raspberries
sugar (see method)
2 Vitamin B¹ tablets
yeast nutrient
yeast (high-alcohol-tolerance)
water to 6 gallons (27 litres)

American

33 lb elderberries
33 lb fresh black Hamburg
   grapes
8 lb bananas
1¾ lb morello cherries
1 lb raspberries
sugar (see method)
2 Vitamin B¹ tablets
yeast nutrient
yeast (high-alcohol-tolerance)
water to 6 gallons

Steam the elderberries, cherries and raspberries in a steam juice extractor. [If you don't have a steamer, heat the fruit in water

to boiling point, then press it to extract the juice — Ed.]
Transfer the juice to a fermentation bin and add the liquid
obtained by simmering the peeled, chopped bananas in water
for a few minutes.

Place all the grapes in boiling water for five minutes, then
destalk but do not crush them (the wine which achieved the
award mentioned below was prepared by fermenting on the
whole grapes). Add the grapes to the fermentation bin and
then adjust the volume to about 6 gallons (27 litres) and the
initial s.g. to about 1.070 with sugar syrup. Be sure to leave
room for later additions of syrup. Allow the must to cool if
necessary, then add the nutrients and an active yeast starter.
[Mr Mitchell uses additional nutrient in this high-alcohol wine,
although ammonium phosphate is perfectly acceptable — Ed.]

Ferment on the pulp for four days from the time when the
cap of fruit has formed, keeping covered and stirring twice
daily. Then strain off the liquid and transfer it to your large
fermenter under air-lock. Each time the specific gravity falls
to 1.010 add 4 oz (110 g) of sugar or ¼ pint (150 ml) of syrup
per gallon (4.5 litres) of wine. Feed the wine in this way until
the desired level of alcohol is reached: with a little care and
patience, 16–18% of alcohol is quite feasible. (Alternatively,
the wine may be siphoned off at s.g. 1.020 and fortified with
vodka.)

When the fermentation is over, rack the wine as necessary
and sulphite as normal. [You may find it helpful to refer to
the information on storage and maturation in Part I of this
book; clearly this is a wine which would benefit from storage
in wood — Ed.] Sweeten the wine as necessary: for a port,
s.g. 1.022 is probably about right; although in the dessert wine
class at the show listed below, the wine was sweetened to s.g.
1.036. It is all really a matter of taste.

Raisin Dessert Wine

MRS M. HAYES OF TODMORDEN WINE CIRCLE

FIRST PRIZE, ROCHDALE ANNUAL COMPETITION 1986

Imperial (Metric)
8 lb (3.6 kg) large raisins
1 Vitamin B¹ tablet
1 tsp pectic enzyme
1 tsp citric acid
yeast and nutrient
water to 1 gallon (4.5 litres)

American
7 lb large raisins
1 Vitamin B¹ tablet
1 tsp pectic enzyme
1 tsp citric acid
yeast and nutrient
water to 1 gallon

[The apparently large quantity of raisins is needed to obtain the body and sugar required for a dessert wine. As Mrs Hayes observes, "the judges' comments at competitions have proved that 8 lb (3.6 kg) is just right." In fact, the weight of raisins used is equivalent to about 32 lb (14.5 kg) of fresh grapes, a figure which reflects the very large amount of grapes needed to make the best and sweetest German white wines: that is to say, those wines produced from grapes which have shrivelled on the vines so that their sugar content is much higher than normal. The wine is not too expensive anyway, especially as a second batch can be made from the fruit pulp in the way described later — Ed.]

Mince the raisins and place them in a fermentation bucket. Add about a gallon (4.5 litres) of water in which a Campden tablet has been dissolved, cover and leave for twenty-four hours. Then add the pectic enzyme, yeast and nutrients. Leave to ferment on the pulp for twenty-one days, keeping well covered with a lid and plastic bag but stirring daily. Then strain off the liquid (using a fine strainer) and transfer it to a demijohn. Top up if necessary, fit an air-lock and allow the fermentation to proceed to completion; this should take just a few days. Rack and stabilize the wine in the normal way and when it has cleared, sweeten it slightly if necessary to obtain a final s.g. of about 1.020. Leave the wine to mature for about one year before use.

Meanwhile, transfer the raisin pulp from the straining bag to a fermentation bucket and add 2 lb (900 g) of sugar dissolved in about 7 pints (4 litres) of water, 1 tsp each of citric acid, pectic enzyme, yeast nutrient and a little extra wine yeast. Cover and leave to ferment for five days, stirring daily. Then strain through a fine mesh into a demijohn, top up if necessary, fit an air-lock and ferment out. Rack and mature as normal.

Raisin and Sultana Wine
(Sweet)

MR E. MEMORY OF OLDHAM WINE CIRCLE
LOCAL CIRCLE PRIZEWINNING WINE

Imperial (Metric)
1 lb (450 g) Muscatel raisins
8 oz (225 g) sultanas
8 oz (225 g) crystal malt
3 lb (1.35 kg) sugar
¼ tsp grape tannin
1 tsp citric acid
1 tsp tartaric acid
1 tsp Pectolase
yeast (general-purpose) and nutrient
water to 1 gallon (4.5 litres)

American
1 lb Muscatel raisins
8 oz sultanas
8 oz crystal malt
2½ lb sugar
¼ tsp grape tannin
1 tsp citric acid
1 tsp tartaric acid
1 tsp Pectolase
yeast (general-purpose) and nutrient
water to 1 gallon

Crush the malt by rolling it under a cloth. Chop or mince the raisins and sultanas, and place them in a pan with 4–5 pints (2.3–2.8 litres) of water. Bring to the boil and slowly add 1 lb (450 g) of sugar, stirred until the sugar has dissolved. Then pour everything into a fermentation bin or bucket and allow to cool to 21°C (70°F). Add the tannin, acid, nutrient, Pectolase and yeast. Mix well, cover, and leave to ferment on the pulp for about ten days, stirring occasionally.

Strain the liquid into a 1 gallon (4.5 litre) demijohn. Add 2 lb (900 g) of sugar dissolved in water, and top up to the neck of the jar. Fit an air-lock and leave in a warm place to ferment. When the fermentation is complete, allow the wine to clear, then rack as necessary. The wine may be sweetened if required. Although it will be ready to drink after four months, it will certainly improve with keeping.

Raspberry Wine
(Sweet)

MRS RENÉE GOLDING OF CHALFONT ST PETER, BUCKINGHAMSHIRE

FIRST PRIZE, RED FRUIT WINE (SWEET), THE NATIONAL SHOW 1986

Imperial (Metric)
3½ lb (1.6 kg) raspberries★
up to 3½ lb (1.6 kg) sugar
  (see method)
1 Vitamin B¹ tablet
Pectolase
yeast starter and nutrient
water to 1 gallon (4.5 litres)

American
3 lb raspberries★
up to 3 lb sugar (see method)

1 Vitamin B¹ tablet
Pectolase
yeast starter and nutrient
water to 1 gallon

★8 oz (225 g) of loganberries may be substituted for 8 oz (225 g) of raspberries.

Crush ripe (but not overripe), sound fruit in a fermentation bucket and add 4 pints (2.3 litres) of cold water in which 1 Campden tablet has been dissolved. Add the Pectolase, cover and leave for twenty-four hours. Then add the yeast starter and allow the pulp fermentation to continue for twenty-four hours, occasionally pressing down the fruit cap.

Next, strain carefully into a demijohn, pressing the fruit pulp very lightly. Add 2 lb (900 g) of sugar dissolved in enough water to bring the volume up to about 7½ pints (4.25 litres); this will leave room for further additions of sugar. Add the nutrient, mix well and fit an air-lock. As the fermentation continues, keep checking the specific gravity, and each time it falls below 1.010, dissolve 2–4 oz (60–120 g) of sugar in the wine. (In the later stages never let the specific gravity rise above 1.020 in case the fermentation ceases.) When the wine has reached its limit of fermentation the final s.g. can be up to 1.025 or even more, according to taste.

When the wine has fallen clear, rack and if necessary top up with water. If the wine has a heavy deposit, it may be better to rack it again into a smaller container [or top up with a similar wine — Ed.] This wine improves after two years, and won this prize when four years old.

Redcurrant Rosé
(Medium Dry)

MRS RENÉE GOLDING OF CHALFONT ST PETER, BUCKINGHAMSHIRE

SECOND PRIZE, MEDIUM DRY ROSÉ CLASS, THE NATIONAL SHOW 1976

Imperial (Metric)
2 lb (900 g) redcurrants
 (topped and tailed)
2 lb (900 g) sugar
1 Vitamin B¹ tablet
Pectolase
yeast nutrient

American
1¾ lb redcurrants (topped
 and tailed)
1¾ lb sugar
1 Vitamin B¹ tablet
Pectolase
yeast nutrient

yeast starter (Chablis or all-
 purpose)
water to 1 gallon (4.5 litres)

yeast starter (Chablis or all-
 purpose)
water to 1 gallon

Prepare the fruit and strip it from the stalks. The redcurrants should be ripe to the bottom of the bunch, but not overripe. Crush the berries and cover them with cold water, then add the pectic enzyme and 1 dissolved Campden tablet. Cover and leave for twenty-four hours. Add a yeast starter and ferment on the pulp for a further twenty-four hours, pressing down the fruit cap occasionally. Strain off the liquid, exerting only the gentlest pressure on the pulp, and add 2 lb (900 g) of sugar. Stir well to dissolve, then add enough water to bring the volume up to 1 gallon (4.5 litres). Add the nutrients, put under air-lock and ferment to dryness. The specific gravity will be about 0.990. Allow the wine to clear, then rack and top up as necessary. The wine is ready in one year but keeps well for a further year or two.

For those who prefer a medium dry rosé, and for exhibiting, the wine can be sweetened before use. Remove about 1 oz (30 g) of wine from a bottle, add one small dessertspoon of sugar and dissolve it completely to give an s.g. reading of 0.995. Fill the bottle with cold water to reduce alcohol. Any risk of refermentation can be avoided by keeping the bottle in a fridge or a cool place for two to three days until it is needed. Alternatively, a few drops of Sweetex can be added with no risk of refermentation and a quite acceptable taste.

Rose Petal Wine
(Dry)

MR ROY SMALES OF NOTTINGHAM

FIRST PRIZE, THE NATIONAL SHOW 1980

Imperial (Metric)
*4 pints (2.3 litres) red rose
  petals*
juice of 2 large lemons
2½ lb (1.15 kg) sugar
1 Vitamin B tablet
1 tsp yeast nutrient
1 tsp pectic enzyme
yeast (general-purpose)
water to 1 gallon (4.5 litres)

American
4 pints red rose petals

juice of 2 large lemons
2 lb sugar
1 Vitamin B tablet
1 tsp yeast nutrient
1 tsp pectic enzyme
yeast (general-purpose)
water to 1 gallon

This wine is better fermented slowly in a cool room; yeasts specially formulated for lower temperatures are available from winemaking shops.

Measure out the required quantity of rose petals, lightly pressed down, in a measuring jug. Then place the petals in a bucket and add the sugar. Pour on 8 pints (4.5 litres) of boiling water and stir until the sugar has dissolved. Cover, leave to cool, then add the other ingredients and the yeast.

After seven days, strain the liquid into a demijohn and leave it to ferment slowly in a cool room until it is finished; this will take about two months.

When the wine has finished fermenting and is more or less clear, siphon it carefully into a fresh demijohn, leaving behind all the sediment. When the wine is fully clear, it is ready for bottling and will take nine months to mature. It should then have a beautiful flowery bouquet.

"Sauternes"

FYLDE AMATEUR WINEMAKERS' GUILD
FIRST PRIZE, FYLDE AMATEUR WINEMAKERS' GUILD SHOW 1981

Imperial (Metric)
8 oz (225 g) sultanas
8 oz (225 g) ripe peeled
  bananas
8 oz (225 g) bottled or canned
  gooseberries
15 oz (450 g) canned apricots
1 pint (550 ml) apple juice
1 tsp dried elderflowers
2½ lb (1.15 kg) sugar
1½ tsp acid blend (citric,
  malic, tartaric)
¼ tsp grape tannin
1 tsp nutrient
1 Vitamin B tablet
1 tsp Pectolase
yeast (Sauternes) starter
water to 1 gallon (4.5 litres)

American
8 oz sultanas
8 oz ripe peeled bananas

8 oz bottled or canned
  gooseberries
12 oz canned apricots
1 pint apple juice
1 tsp dried elderflowers
2 lb sugar
1½ tsp acid blend (citric,
  malic, tartaric)
¼ tsp grape tannin
1 tsp nutrient
1 Vitamin B tablet
1 tsp Pectolase
yeast (Sauternes) starter
water to 1 gallon

Chop the sultanas and place them in a 2 gallon (9 litres) poly-thene bucket with 2 pints (1.2 litres) of boiling water. Slice the bananas, and simmer the pieces in 1 pint (550 ml) of water for thirty minutes. Strain the resulting liquid into the bucket (the banana flesh is discarded). Add the sugar and stir until it has dissolved, then add the tinned fruit and apple juice. Make the volume up to 1 gallon (4.5 litres) with cool, boiled water. Allow the must to cool if necessary and then add the dried elderflowers, pectic enzyme, acids, tannin and nutrients, toge-ther with the yeast starter. Cover and leave in a warm place to ferment for seven days, stirring daily.

Next, strain through a nylon mesh bag into a 1-gallon (4.5-litre) demijohn, top up with cool, boiled water and fit an airlock. When the specific gravity has fallen to 1.020, add 1 Campden tablet and 1 sorbate tablet. One month later rack the wine off the sediment, filter if necessary, and add 1 oz (30 g) of glycerine. Bottle and leave to mature.

Sherry

The flavour of sherry comes chiefly from the presence of certain chemical compounds known as "aldehydes" in the wine. Any normal wine which contains these compounds would be considered ruined, for they impart a distinctive flavour and taste which is only appropriate in a wine compounded for use as a sherry. Where, then, do these aldehydes come from? There are in fact two rather different ways in which they can be formed.

The first, and certainly the easier of the two for the home winemaker, is a process called oxidation. This is a slow chemical reaction which will happen naturally in any wine exposed to the air; it involves the transformation of alcohol to aldehyde along with the darkening of the wine. Oxidation is easily achieved: one simply plugs the incompletely filled storage vessel containing the wine with cotton wool so that air has free access to the wine. Over a period of time, the wine will darken and develop the characteristic sherry nose and taste. When this has developed to a satisfactory extent the wine is, generally speaking, sweetened to produce one of the rich, sweet, dark "cream", "oloroso" or "brown" sherries so popular in England. A commercial Spanish wine intended for this purpose is often fortified before it is allowed to oxidize, so that it also has that characteristic sherry strength and warmth. The home winemaker, however, has the option of fortifying his wine like the commercial producers do, or achieving the highest possible alcohol level during fermentation by "feeding" the sugar in small doses. In fact, as you can see from the recipes for sweet sherry reprinted later in this book, the chosen procedure varies quite a lot, but the end result is always the same.

Pale sherries, on the other hand, develop in a different way. Once again the fermented wine is racked into an incompletely filled container, but this time the oxidation is prevented by the growth of a special type of yeast called a "flor". This flor makes its appearance between six weeks and a year after the racking. It forms as a thin, greyish film on the top of the wine or under the surface, and consists of yeast cells derived from those responsible for the main fermentation. The difference is that the flor needs oxygen to develop: so much so that although the container is left open to the air as it is in the production of dark sherry, this time the yeast flor absorbs all the oxygen and prevents the wine from oxidizing directly. Instead the yeast will itself form aldehydes as a by-product of its metabolism, giving a pale sherry that still has a true sherry nose and taste.

Usually such pale sherries are dry, although in recent years the "pale cream" sherry, which is slightly sweet, has become very popular. In any case, both fortification and sweetening of a pale sherry must be done after the first fermentation and flor formation and dispersal are complete, since sherry flor will only form in a dry wine containing 12–15% of alcohol.

One other point worth noting about sherry production is the importance of gypsum (this is simply calcium sulphate and can be obtained from any winemaking shop). Particularly in dry sherry production, the gypsum helps develop the flavour and reduces the acidity of the must, thereby helping to produce the conditions needed for the formation of a sherry flor. Often it is used in conjunction with cream of tartar, in which case care must be taken to ensure that the cream of tartar dissolves completely. Gypsum does not, however, appear to be absolutely essential in the production of dark sweet sherries.

Dry Apple Sherry

Imperial (Metric)	**American**
3½ pints (2 litres) pure apple juice	3½ pints pure apple juice
½ can (500 g) sherry-type grape concentrate	½ pint sherry-type grape concentrate
2 lb (900 g) sugar	1¾ lb sugar
1 oz (30 g) gypsum (calcium sulphate)	1 oz gypsum (calcium sulphate)
½ oz (15 g) cream of tartar	½ oz cream of tartar
½ tsp tartaric acid	½ tsp tartaric acid
sherry flor yeast and nutrient (e.g. Gervin brand)	sherry flor yeast and nutrient (e.g. Gervin brand)
water to 1 gallon (4.5 litres)	water to 1 gallon

Mix the fruit juice and concentrate with half the sugar and enough water to produce a total volume of 6½ pints (3.7 litres). Add the acid, cream of tartar and nutrients, and stir until the cream of tartar has dissolved. Then introduce a vigorous sherry yeast starter of not more than ¾ pint (425 ml) volume. Transfer to a demijohn and fit an air-lock. Ferment for three weeks, or until the specific gravity has fallen to 1.000, then dissolve the remaining sugar in the wine and ferment to completion.

When the fermentation has finished, allow the yeast to settle for one week before racking into a clean demijohn. (Do not add a Campden tablet unless you know that the sherry yeast you are using can tolerate the sulphite.) Plug the neck of the jar, which should not be more than seven-eighths full, with a sterile cotton-wool plug and leave the wine undisturbed in a cool, dry place (15–17°C/59–62°F). The formation of the flor may take weeks or months; it may appear as a film on the surface of the wine or it may be submerged.

Leave the wine until the flor has disintegrated and formed a sediment on the bottom of the jar; this may take as long as three years. It can then be bottled. (If no flor has formed after six months, sweeten the wine to taste and bottle. It should still have a sherry-like flavour.) The wine is best stored for nine months before use and will certainly improve with keeping.

Sherry
(Amontillado Style)

MR JOHN HOLGATE OF HATCH END, LONDON

FIRST PRIZE, SHERRY STYLE FORTIFIED CLASS,
MIDDLESEX FEDERATION SHOW 1983

Imperial (Metric)
For 4 gallons (18 litres):
*1 lb (450 g) dried rosehip
  shells*
  *or 8 lb (3.6 kg) fresh
    rosehips*
2 lb (900 g) raisins
1 lb (450 g) figs
1 lb (450 g) dates
8 lb (3.6 kg) sugar (approx.)
*4 oz (110 g) gypsum (calcium
  sulphate)*
2 oz (60 g) cream of tartar
1 oz (30 g) tartaric acid
Pectolase

American

12 oz dried rosehip shells

or 6½ lb fresh rosehips

1¾ lb raisins
12 oz figs
12 oz dates
7 lb sugar (approx.)
*4 oz gypsum (calcium
  sulphate)*
2 oz cream of tartar
1 oz tartaric acid
Pectolase

good sherry yeast and nutrient
   (e.g. Vierka liquid sherry
   yeast)
water to 4 gallons (18 litres)

good sherry yeast and nutrient
   (e.g. Vierka liquid sherry
   yeast)
water to 4 gallons

Notes:

(i) The fermentation and bulk maturation of this wine must take place in the presence of air, for example 4 gallons (18 litres) in a 5-gallon (22.5-litre) bucket covered with a lid, or in a 5-gallon (22.5-litre) fermenter with the opening plugged with cotton wool, not an air-lock.

(ii) The wine is racked only once at the end of fermentation, and is then bulk matured for about six months or until the taste is satisfactory; it is then bottled.

(iii) You must use a good sherry yeast: Vierka liquid sherry yeast is recommended.

(iv) For a cream sherry, use 1 lb (450 g) of dried prunes instead of the dates, and add the juice from 4 lb (1.8 kg) of simmered ripe bananas. Also, replace 3–4 lb (1.35–1.8 kg) of the white sugar with the same amount of light brown sugar.

Method:

Prepare the sherry yeast in a starter bottle before preparing the rest of the ingredients.

Mince the raisins, dates and figs and put them in about 1 gallon (4.5 litres) of water with the rosehip shells. Bring to the boil and *simmer* for twenty minutes. Allow to cool, then transfer fruit and liquid to a 5-gallon (22.5-litre) fermentation bin. Add all the other ingredients and the sugar dissolved in enough water to produce a volume of 4 gallons (8 litres) at an initial gravity of 1.110. (About 8 lb or 3.6 kg of sugar will be needed.) Ensure the must is at 18–24°C (65–75°F) and then add the yeast starter.

Ferment on the pulp for about a week, keeping covered and stirring daily. Then strain off the liquid and transfer it to a 5-

gallon (22.5-litre) fermenter, but do not fit an air-lock: use a cotton-wool plug instead. Allow the fermentation to continue until the specific gravity falls to 1.000, then start "feeding" the wine with sugar; this is done by adding about 4 oz (110 g) per gallon (4.5 litres) each time the s.g. level falls to 1.000. This will produce the maximum possible alcohol.

When the fermentation has finally ended, rack the wine into a clean 5-gallon (22.5-litre) container with a cotton-wool plug and leave it for about six months or until the taste is satisfactory. At this stage, fine with *gelatine* finings and again a few days later with Bentonite. Although the wine will clear without the finings, the use of about 5 ml of 1% gelatine solution per gallon (4.5 litres) will remove some of the tannin content. As this usually leaves the wine hazy, it is necessary to finish the fining process by the use of Bentonite.

Finally, the wine can be bottled and fortified by adding 4–5 fl oz (120–150 ml) of vodka per bottle. It is then suitable for the fortified wine class in the show.

Sultana and Date Wine
(Sherry-Type Sweet Wine)

MR T. CORDWELL OF DERBY

FRIST PRIZE, EAST MIDLANDS FEDERATION SHOW 1982

Imperial (Metric)
For 2 gallons (9 litres):
4 lb (1.8 kg) sultanas
2 lb (900 g) dates
1 can (1 kg) concentrated
   white grape juice
8 oz (225 g) bananas
sugar (see method)
1 tsp citric acid

American

3½ lb sultanas
1¾ lb dates
1 pint concentrated white
   grape juice
8 oz bananas
sugar (see method)
1 tsp citric acid

2 tsp pectic enzyme
2 Vitamin B tablets
1 tsp yeast nutrient
yeast (Madeira)
water to 2 gallons (9 litres)

2 tsp pectic enzyme
2 Vitamin B tablets
1 tsp yeast nutrient
yeast (Madeira)
water to 2 gallons

Prepare the yeast starter. Stone the dates and chop them with the sultanas, then simmer both these fruits in sufficient water for about twenty minutes. Then place the fruit and liquid in a 3-gallon (14-litre) fermentation bucket and add the citric acid. Cover and allow to cool overnight.

Simmer the peeled, chopped bananas with sufficient water for fifteen minutes, then strain the liquor only into the bucket. At the correct temperature for fermentation add the nutrients, enzyme, and the active yeast preparation and make the volume up to 1½ gallons (7 litres) with cool, boiled water. Cover and leave to ferment on the pulp for four days, stirring daily.

Strain the liquid off the pulp into a clean bucket and add the grape concentrate. Make up the volume to 2 gallons (9 litres) with cool, boiled water, and leave to ferment for another three days, keeping the bucket covered. Then split the wine into two demijohns and fit air-locks. Continue the fermentation until the s.g. falls to 1.010, then dissolve 4 oz (110 g) of sugar in each jar. Repeat the process as many times as possible when the gravity falls to 1.010.

When the fermentation finally ends, rack the wine into clean demijohns and move them to a cool place to clear. Rack as necessary. When the wine is perfectly clear, sweeten with sugar until the s.g. reaches 1.030, then add 3 dessertspoonfuls of glycerine per demijohn.

Controlled oxidation: Remove the liquid from the air-lock and twist cotton wool into the opening. (Replace the cap if you are using a straight-sided, two-part air-lock). Test the wine every two weeks until the appropriate level of oxidation for a sherry flavour has been achieved. Do not leave too long or the flavour will be ruined. Then seal the demijohns with tight fitting bungs (not rubber) and mature for eighteen months to two years.

Sweet Oloroso
(Sherry)

MR J.K. WALKER OF NEWLANDS WINE CIRCLE

SECOND PRIZE, SWEET SHERRY CLASS,
NORTH-WEST FEDERATION SHOW

Imperial (Metric)
4 lb (1.8 kg) parsnips
1 lb (450 g) raisins
8 oz (225 g) dried apricots
8 oz (225 g) prunes
1 lb (430 g) bananas
1 pint (350 ml) concentrated
  grape juice (sherry-type)
sugar (see method)
3 tsp tartaric acid
pectic enzyme
sherry yeast and nutrient
water to 1 gallon (4.5 litres)

American
3½ lb parsnips
1 lb raisins
8 oz dried apricots
8 oz prunes
1 lb bananas
1 pint concentrated grape juice
  (sherry-type)
sugar (see method)
3 tsp tartaric acid
pectic enzyme
sherry yeast and nutrient
water to 1 gallon

[Although this recipe needs time and patience, the results are well worthwhile. In a "blind" tasting, one of the better batches of this wine could not be distinguished from a Spanish commercial sherry — Ed.]

Harvest the parsnips after they have been nipped by the frosts in January. Scrub and peel them, cut them into chunks and simmer in about 3½ pints (2 litres) of water until they are just tender. This will take about ten minutes; do not over-cook or the wine may not clear. Simmer the peeled and chopped bananas in about 1 pint (600 ml) of water for thirty minutes. Strain the liquid from both parsnips and bananas onto the other washed and chopped fruit in a fermentation bin or bucket. Allow to cool, then add the pectic enzyme, cover and leave for twenty-four hours.

Next, add the acid, nutrient and 1 lb (450 g) of sugar dissolved in about ½ pint (300 ml) of water. Check that the must is at the correct fermentation temperature and add the yeast. Ferment on the pulp for about seven days, keeping well covered and stirring daily.

Strain the liquid into a demijohn and mix in the concentrate. Fit an air-lock and leave to ferment for three days before adding another 8 oz (225 g) of sugar as sugar syrup; this will ensure that the sugar can be mixed easily and completely into the wine. [Use either a standard syrup made from 2 lb (900 g) of sugar dissolved in 1 pint (350 ml) of water, in which case ½ pint (300 ml) of the resulting syrup will contain 8 oz (450 g) of sugar; or simply dissolve the sugar in the smallest possible quantity of water before adding it to the wine — Ed.] Refit the air-lock and leave to ferment.

As the fermentation continues, keep checking the specific gravity. Each time the s.g. falls to 1.010 add 4 oz (110 g) of sugar or ¼ pint (150 ml) of sugar syrup. Ferment out as much sugar as possible to obtain the highest possible alcohol level: an *overall* total of 3 lb (1.35 kg) or more is a good achievement. [A consistent fermentation temperature of about 21°C (70°F) is essential — Ed.]

When the fermentation finally ends, allow the sediment to settle for about three weeks before racking the wine into a clean demijohn. (If the wine forms a heavy deposit, a second racking should be c. rried out about two weeks later.)

Sweeten the wine with sugar syrup to raise the specific gravity to about 1.025, or to personal taste. Plug the neck of the jar with cotton wool and keep the level of the wine between the shoulder and the neck of the jar. This will allow the air free access to the wine and so develop the oxidation necessary for a sherry flavour. This may develop in less than one year or take as long as three years. When the wine is ready, it can be fortified with commercial spirit to give about 20% alcohol if required, and then bottled.

Sherry Type Wine
(Sweet)

FYLDE AMATEUR WINEMAKERS' GUILD

FIRST PRIZE, FYLDE WINEMAKERS' SHOW 1984

Imperial (Metric)	**American**
8 oz (225 g) raisins	6 oz raisins
8 oz (225 g) figs	6 oz figs
8 oz (225 g) dates	6 oz dates
4 oz (110 g) dried rosehips	4 oz dried rosehips
8 oz (225 g) peeled, ripe bananas	8 oz peeled, ripe bananas
2 lb (900 g) demerara sugar	1¾ lb demerara sugar
1 tsp tartaric acid	1 tsp tartaric acid
1 tsp Pectolase	1 tsp Pectolase
1 tsp yeast nutrient	1 tsp yeast nutrient
sherry yeast starter	sherry yeast starter
water to 1 gallon (4.5 litres)	water to 1 gallon

Chop the raisins, figs, rosehips and dates and place them in a 2-gallon (9-litre) plastic bucket with 2 pints (1.2 litres) of boiling water. Slice the bananas and simmer the pieces for thirty minutes in 1 pint (350 ml) of water, then strain the liquor into the bucket with the other fruit. (The banana flesh is discarded.)

Add the demerara sugar and stir until dissolved, then make up to the gallon (4.5 litres) with cool, boiled water. Check that the must is at normal fermentation temperature, then add the pectic enzyme, acid, nutrient and yeast starter. Leave to ferment in a warm place for seven days, stirring daily and keeping covered.

After one week, strain through a nylon bag into a 1-gallon (4.5-litre) demijohn. Do not top up the jar. Fit an air-lock and leave for one month. Then dissolve 1½ lb (700 g) of sugar in ¾ pint (450 ml) of boiling water and simmer for a few minutes; add this syrup to the wine a few ounces (about 100 g) at a time throughout the following month until the fermentation can proceed no further. Then rack the wine off the sediment and add 1 sorbate tablet and 1 Campden tablet. The air-space should remain to allow oxidation of the wine. Plug the top of the demijohn with cotton wool.

After six months the wine may be racked off and sweetened to taste. Bottle and mature as normal.

Sloe Wine
(Dry)

MR G.A. BROWN OF CARNFORTH, LANCASHIRE

FIRST PRIZE, CATON SHOW 1967

Imperial (Metric)
1¼ lb (550 g) sloes
2 lb (900 g) raisins
2½ lb (1.15 kg) sugar
1 tsp pectic enzyme
1 tsp yeast nutrient
yeast (general-purpose)
water to 1 gallon (4.5 litres)

American
1¼ lb sloes
1¾ lb raisins
2 lb sugar
1 tsp pectic enzyme
1 tsp yeast nutrient
yeast (general-purpose)
water to 1 gallon

Lightly liquidize the raisins in 1 pint (550 ml) of water. Pour 3 pints (1.7 litres) of boiling water over the sloes, add the raisins and leave overnight. Then add the yeast starter, nutrient and pectic enzyme; ferment on the pulp for two or three days, keeping covered and stirring daily.

Strain off the pulp and transfer the liquid to a demijohn, adding the sugar dissolved in enough water to bring the volume up to 1 gallon (4.5 litres). Fit an air-lock and ferment to dryness. Rack as normal.

Sloe, Blackberry and Elderberry Wine
(Dessert Wine)

MR AND MRS T. NICHOLLS OF OKEHAMPTON, DEVON

FIRST PRIZE, SOMERSET ASSOCIATION OF AMATEUR WINEMAKERS' SHOW 1979

Imperial (Metric)

For 2 gallons (9 litres):
2 lb (900 g) sloes
1 lb (450 g) blackberries
1 lb (450 g) elderberries
2 lb (900 g) ripe bananas
2 lb (900 g) raisins (black)
2 pints (1.2 litres)
   concentrated red grape juice
sugar (see method)
2 Vitamin B¹ tablets
pectic enzyme
yeast starter and nutrient
water to 2 gallons (9 litres)

American

1¾ lb sloes
1 lb blackberries
1 lb elderberries
1¾ lb ripe bananas
1¾ lb raisins (black)
2 pints concentrated red grape
   juice
sugar (see method)
2 Vitamin B¹ tablets
pectic enzyme
yeast starter and nutrient
water to 2 gallons

Pressure-cook the bananas in 2 pints (1.2 litres) of water for five minutes at 15 lb (7 kg) pressure. Pour the hot liquid thus obtained over the pulped fruit and minced raisins. (Take care not to break the sloe stones.) Allow to cool, then add the enzyme, nutrient and yeast, and enough water to bring the volume up to about 12 pints (7 litres). Ferment on the pulp for four days, keeping well covered and stirring twice daily.

Strain into a 2-gallon (9-litre) fermentation vessel [or two 1-gallon demijohns — Ed] and add the concentrated grape juice. Mix well. Fit an air-lock and leave to ferment until the fermentation slows or the specific gravity falls to 1.004. Then "feed" the wine with sugar syrup made by dissolving 2 lb (900 g) of sugar in 1 pint (550 ml) of water; add about ¼ pint (150 ml) of syrup each time the s.g. falls to 1.005. Mix well. When the fermentation finally ceases, rack the wine, fine or filter as necessary, and mature appropriately. Sweeten as required.

Sultana and Raisin Wine
(Dry)

MR MICHAEL DICKINSON OF LIPHOOK WINE CIRCLE

PRIZEWINNING WINE, MID-SOUTHERN WINE FESTIVAL 1971

Imperial (Metric)	American
1 lb (500 g) white grapes	1 lb white grapes
1 lb (500 g) sultanas	12 oz sultanas
1 lb (500 g) raisins	12 oz raisins
2 oranges	2 oranges
2½ lb (1 kg) sugar	2¼ lb sugar
pectic enzyme	pectic enzyme
yeast and nutrient (sherry-type)	yeast and nutrient (sherry-type)
water to 1 gallon (4.5 litres)	water to 1 gallon

Prepare a yeast starter bottle forty-eight hours before making the wine. (Use the juice of the oranges, 1 tbsp of sugar, 1 tbsp of malt extract, yeast and nutrient and about 1 cupful of water. Place all these ingredients in a sterilized bottle, shake to dissolve the sugar and malt extract, plug the neck with cotton wool and leave for about forty-eight hours in a warm place.)

Mince the raisins and sultanas, pulp the grapes, and put the fruit into a fermentation bin or bucket. Add the sugar and 6 pints (3.5 litres) of boiling water. Stir to dissolve the sugar and leave to cool, then add the contents of the starter bottle and pectic enzyme. Stir well, cover and leave to ferment in a constant temperature of 18–21°C (65–70°F) for at least two weeks, stirring twice daily.

Strain the liquid into a fermentation jar and make up to 1 gallon (4.5 litres) by adding cold water. Fit an air-lock and maintain the same temperature until the wine has fermented to dryness. Rack the wine, add 1 crushed Campden tablet, and store for at least one year, preferably in a cool place (10°C/ 50°F). A deposit will form, but the wine can be siphoned into clean wine bottles.

This is a wine you will be proud of, and can be compared favourably with a lot of the cheaper sherries. It is easy to make, and the ingredients can be multiplied by three to make 3 gallons (13.5 litres) at a time.

Summer Fruits Rosé Wine
(Medium Dry)

DR PHILIP DRANSFIELD OF GELLIFOR, CLWYD

FIRST PRIZE, THE NATIONAL SHOW 1976

Imperial (Metric)
For 5 gallons (22.5 litres):
10 pints (5.5 litres) mixed
rose petals

American

10 pints mixed rose petals

10 lb (4.6 kg) ripe
  gooseberries (preferably red)
2 lb (900 g) raspberries
1 lb (450 g) strawberries
2 cans (2 kg) concentrated
  white or rosé grape juice
9 lb (4 kg) sugar
pectic enzyme
yeast (Mosel or Port) and
  nutrient
water to 5 gallons (22.5 litres)

8 lb ripe gooseberries
  (preferably red)
2 lb raspberries
1 lb strawberries
2 pints concentrated white or
  rosé grape juice
7½ lb sugar
pectic enzyme
yeast (Mosel or Port) and
  nutrient
water to 5 gallons

Pick the rose petals when the roses are full blown. Spread them out on a sheet in the sun for thirty minutes so that any insects will disperse, then place the petals in a large covered bin or bucket and add 3 gallons (14 litres) of water at about 60°C — the temperature of hot tea. Should you have them available, about 10 pints (5.5 litres) of tender vine prunings can be included with the rose petals. Cover and leave for two days.

Strain off the liquid and add it to the crushed fruit. Add the pectic enzyme, yeast nutrient and 5 dissolved Campden tablets (or the equivalent). Soak for three days, keeping the mixture covered. Next, strain off the juices and wash the pulp with water to get 4½ gallons (20 litres) of must. Return the must to the bucket and add the sugar and grape concentrate. Ensure that this dissolves completely, then add the yeast. Ferment in the bucket for three days, skimming off any pulp which may have passed through the strainer, but otherwise keeping it covered. Then transfer the wine to a 5-gallon (22.5-litre) vessel with an air-lock and go through the normal fermentation and racking procedures.

This wine is at its best in about six to eight months, and later at eighteen months to two years. It will probably finish fermenting dry, but can be adjusted to medium dry immediately before drinking or showing; the best sweetener is natural strength red or white grape juice.

Dr Dransfield makes some interesting observations on rosé wines. Often, he says, a prizewinning rosé wine can only be achieved by judicious blending: for example, by blending the original wine with very pale, light rosés derived from gooseberries to lighten the body and balance; and sometimes with heavy rosés based on apple, blackberry, elderberry and so forth to restore body to the wine. However, the recipe shown above has produced a wine which is not only good in its own right, but which has also been a major component of many prizewinning blends.

Summer Fruits Social Wine
(Medium Sweet)

DR PHILIP DRANSFIELD OF GELLIFOR, CLWYD

RED SOCIAL WINE CLASS PRIZEWINNER, MID-CHESHIRE SHOW 1978

Imperial (Metric)
For 5 gallons (22.5 litres):
12 lb (5.4 kg) redcurrants★
4 lb (1.8 kg) raspberries
4 lb (1.8 kg) strawberries
2 cans (2 kg) concentrated red grape juice (Solvino)
11 lb (5 kg) sugar
Pectolase
yeast (Tokay) and nutrient
water to 5 gallons (22.5 litres)

American
10 lb redcurrants★
3½ lb raspberries
3½ lb strawberries
2 pints concentrated red grape juice (Solvino)
9 lb sugar
Pectolase
yeast (Tokay) and nutrient
water to 5 gallons

★To be very successful, and not over-burdened with acidity, the fruit must be very ripe. The redcurrants must be so ripe that the pips gleam out at you through the skins! If you can't get hold of 12 lb (5.4 kg) of good, ripe redcurrants, one alternative would be to use a mixture of 4 lb (1.8 kg) of ripe blackcurrants and 8 lb (3.6 kg) of gooseberries instead (preferably red gooseberries, but green ones would do).

Crush the fruit into 3 gallons (14 litres) of cold water (hot water can be used if the fruit has been stored in the freezer). If you wish, 6 pints (3.5 litres) of rose petals may also be included at this stage. Add the yeast nutrient, Pectolase and 5 dissolved Campden tablets. Cover and soak for three days. Then strain off the juices and wash the pulp with water to get 4½ gallons (20 litres) of must. The pulp can be used again to make a second batch of wine.

Dissolve the grape concentrate and 11 lb (5 kg) of sugar in the must and then introduce the yeast. Ferment in the 5-gallon (22.5-litre) bucket for three more days, skimming off any pulp which may have passed through the first straining, but otherwise keeping covered. Then transfer the wine to a 5-gallon (22.5-litre) fermentation vessel with an air-lock; the fermentation is conducted at a temperature of 18–21°C (65–70°F). Go through the normal fermentation and racking procedures.

If the wine is stated in July or August, the fermentation will slow down as autumn temperatures prevail. If you are lucky, the wine will stop bright and clear with enough sugar left in it. Alternatively, of course, it may be fermented to dryness and then sweetened, but it does appear to lose some fruitiness if it goes dry.

This wine is best drunk at Christmas the year it is made when fresh and fruity, or after keeping it for eighteen months to two years. Dr Dransfield used this wine as a fruity base for a blend which took the prize shown above.

Summer Fruits Social Wine (2)

MR PATRICK DRANSFIELD OF GELLIFOR, CLWYD

Imperial (Metric)
1 lb (450 g) redcurrants

American
12 oz redcurrants

1 lb (450 g) gooseberries
8 oz (225 g) strawberries
8 oz (225 g) raspberries
½ pint (300 ml) concentrated
  red grape juice
4 pints (2.3 litres) bramble
  tips
2¼ lb (1 kg) sugar
Pectolase
yeast and nutrient
water to 1 gallon (4.5 litres)

12 oz gooseberries
8 oz strawberries
8 oz raspberries
½ pint concentrated red grape
  juice
4 pints bramble tips

1¾ lb sugar
Pectolase
yeast and nutrient
water to 1 gallon

This is a variation on the Summer Fruits Social Wine by Dr Philip Dransfield. The method is essentially the same, but do remember to use the correct quantities of ingredients (including the appropriate number of Campden tablets).

Summer Punch

DR PHILIP DRANSFIELD OF GELLIFOR, CLWYD

This will not win any show prizes, but it certainly will be a success on warm summer evenings.

Take two parts of wine — the Summer Fruits Social Wine and the Summer Rosé are obvious candidates, but any other combination of sound red and white wines will do — and one part of sparkling cider. This can be dry, medium or sweet according to the nature of the wine used and your own preference. Add some blackcurrant cordial to give extra fruitiness and colour. Sharpen, if necessary, with orange or curaçao essence, and garnish with citrus fruits and fresh herbs if desired; lemon balm and borage are very suitable. Serve by the half-pint or Viertel (quarter-litre), from a silver punch bowl if possible.

Tea Wine
(Sweet)

MR M.E. HART OF THREE RIVERS WINE CIRCLE

BEST SWEET WINE IN SHOW, ESSEX WINEMAKERS' FEDERATION
SHOW 1985

Imperial (Metric)
6 tea-bags (Earl Grey, Assam
  or similar)
1 lb (450 g) sultanas
2 lemons
3 lb (1.35 kg) sugar
yeast and nutrient
water to 1 gallon (4.5 litres)

American
6 tea-bags (Earl Grey, Assam
  or similar)
12 oz sultanas
2 lemons
2½ lb sugar
yeast and nutrient
water to 1 gallon

Infuse the tea bags in 2 pints (1.2 litres) of boiling water. Allow to stand for ten minutes, then remove the tea-bags. Meanwhile, make a sugar syrup by boiling 1½ lb (700 g) of sugar in 3½ pints (2 litres) of water. Mix both liquids in a fermentation bucket.

Wash the sultanas in hot water to remove the oil film. Discard the water, chop the sultanas and add them to the fermentation bucket.

Peel the lemons thinly so that no pith adheres to the rind, then simmer the peel in 1 pint (550 ml) of boiling water for fifteen minutes to extract the "zest". Add both rinds and water to the fermentation bucket, together with the juice of the lemons, discarding flesh and pips. When the bucket is cool, add yeast and nutrient. Ferment for seven days, keeping well covered and stirring daily.

Strain into a demijohn. Boil 2 pints (1.2 litres) of water with 1½ lb (700 g) of sugar and when the solution is cool add it to the jar. Fit a fermentation lock and ferment out at a steady temperature of 15–20°C (60–70°F). When the fermentation has finished, rack into a clean jar, top up with boiled water, add a Campden tablet and move to a cool place. Bottle when clear.

Tea and Raisin Social Wine

MR AND MRS T. NICHOLLS OF OKEHAMPTON, DEVON
FIRST PRIZE, WHITE SOCIAL WINE CLASS, SOUTH WESTERN
COUNTIES WINEMAKERS' FEDERATION SHOW 1976

Imperial (Metric)
For 2 gallons (9 litres):
½ oz (15 g) tea
*1 pint (550 ml) concentrated
  white grape juice*
2 lb (900 g) sugar
2 lb (900 g) minced raisins
2 oranges (medium size)
3½ tsp citric acid
2 Vitamin B¹ tablets
pectic enzyme
yeast and nutrient
water to 2 gallons (9 litres)

American
½ oz tea
*1 pint concentrated white
  grape juice*
1¾ lb sugar
1¾ lb minced raisins
2 oranges (medium size)
3½ tsp citric acid
2 Vitamin B¹ tablets
pectic enzyme
yeast and nutrient
water to 2 gallons

Make 12 pints (7 litres) of tea using the ½ oz (15 g) of tea. Pour the hot tea through a fine strainer on to the minced raisins, being careful to exclude tea-leaves from the must. Add the thinly pared rind of the oranges, ensuring that no white pith is included, and allow to cool. Then add the nutrient, acid, enzyme and yeast starter. Ferment on the pulp for three days, keeping well covered and stirring at least once a day. Then strain into a 2-gallon (9-litre) fermentation vessel [or two 1-gallon demijohns — Ed] and add the concentrate. Fit air-locks.

Dissolve 2 lb (900 g) of sugar in 1 pint (550 ml) of water and use this to "feed" the wine, adding ¼ pint (150 ml) of syrup each time the fermentation slows or the s.g. falls to 1.005.

When the fermentation is finally complete, stabilize and rack as normal, fining or filtering as necessary. Sweeten with sugar syrup as needed.

This wine has achieved "Highly Commended" only seven weeks after being made. At seven months of age it took the prize shown above.

Note: For a dessert wine, add 4 lb (1.8 kg) of minced fresh rosehips or 1 lb (450 g) of dried rosehips to the liquor obtained by pressure-cooking 2 lb (900 g) of bananas at 15 lb (7 kg) pressure for five minutes. Then add this to the must and ferment on the pulp for four days.

Vermouth
(Medium Red)

MR AND MRS T. STEWARD OF TAMESIDE WINE CIRCLE

FIRST PRIZE, MEDIUM TO SWEET APERITIF CLASS,
NORTH-WEST FEDERATION SHOW 1985

Imperial (Metric)

1¾ pints (1 litre) mixed fruit juice
1¾ pints (1 litre) red grape juice (Solvino)
2¼ lb (1 kg) sugar
2 tsp tartaric acid
1 tsp Pectolase
1 tsp Tronozymol nutrient
2 Vitamin B¹ tablets
yeast (Gervin Number 3)
water to 1 gallon (4.5 litres)

American

1¾ pints mixed fruit juice
1¾ pints red grape juice (Solvino)
1¾ lb sugar
2 tsp tartaric acid
1 tsp Pectolase
1 tsp Tronozymol nutrient
2 Vitamin B¹ tablets
yeast (Gervin Number 3)
water to 1 gallon

Put the fruit juice (the winning recipe used a carton of Marks and Spencer's mixed fruit juice), sugar and 3½ pints (2 litres) of cold water into a sterilized bucket and stir until the sugar has dissolved. Add the grape juice, Pectolase, acid, nutrient and an active yeast starter — preferably Gervin brand. Cover and ferment in the bucket for two days, stirring three times daily, then transfer to a 1-gallon (4.5-litre) demijohn and add the Vitamin B[1] tablets. Fit an air-lock and ferment for four to five weeks or until the fermentation ends. Allow the wine to clear then rack and taste; sweeten if necessary. The wine should be medium sweet.

Vermouth
(White)

See: Grapefruit and Orange Aperitif
Orange Vermouth
Orange and Grapefruit Aperitif

White Elderberry Wine
(Dry Table Wine)

MR R.C. PENNINGTON OF KENDAL, CUMBRIA

FIRST PRIZE, WHITE DRY TABLE WINE,
KENDAL WINEMAKERS' CIRCLE SHOW 1985

[Everyone knows the red variety of elderberry, but perhaps less well-known is the fact that elderberries also come in white- and yellow-berried varieties. These are somewhat rare, but both can be used to make white wine, the white berries being possibly a little better. Neither berry turns red, but both have a sweet taste when ripe. A word of caution, here, though: please be sure that what you are using is indeed the elderberry, and not something poisonous. If you are in any doubt at all *do not* try Mr Pennington's recipe — Ed.]

Imperial (Metric)	**American**
2 lb (450 g) ripe white or yellow elderberries	1 lb ripe white or yellow elderberries
1¾ pints (1 litre) natural-strength white grape juice	1¾ pints natural-strength white grape juice
2 lb (900 g) sugar	1¾ lb sugar
1 tsp tartaric acid	1 tsp tartaric acid
pectic enzyme	pectic enzyme
yeast (Hock) and nutrient	yeast (Hock) and nutrient
water to 1 gallon (4.5 litres)	water to 1 gallon

Crush the elderberries and pour on 5 pints (2.8 litres) of cold water in which 1 Campden tablet has been dissolved. Add the grape juice, acid and pectic enzyme. Stir and cover, then leave for twenty-four hours. Next add the sugar, nutrient and yeast as a vigorous starter. Cover and leave to ferment on the pulp for three days, stirring twice daily. Then strain into a demi-john, top up if necessary and fit an air-lock. When the fermentation is complete, rack off the sediment and add 1 crushed Campden tablet. Ready after nine to twelve months.

Appendix

The Hydrometer and its Uses in Winemaking

The hydrometer is made up of a glass or plastic tube with a bulb at one end and a graduated scale at the other. When it is placed in a liquid, it floats with the scale protruding above the liquid's surface. The specific gravity of the liquid can then be read off the scale. But what does this mean?

Specific gravity, or s.g., is a measure of a liquid's thickness or density compared to that of pure water. Pure water weighs one gram per cubic centimetre, so it is said to have an s.g. of 1.000. As sugar is dissolved in water, the water (or, rather, the sugar solution) becomes more dense, in other words its specific gravity rises. This means that one can measure the s.g. of a must and discover how much sugar it contains. The information needed to work this out is shown in Table 2. This table also shows the percentage alcohol by volume which can be produced for a given weight of sugar in a must, assuming that the yeast ferments all the sugar to alcohol. This figure is shown in the "potential alcohol" column.

The instructions for using a hydrometer are always included with the instrument and will not be repeated here. One important point, however, is that any fruit pulp in suspension will affect the hydrometer reading, so when you are testing a must, the liquid should be relatively clear, and if necessary strained through a fine sieve.

In practical terms, of course, one is often faced with a must the volume of which is not exactly one gallon (4.5 litres). Table 1 is an illustration of how the hydrometer can be used in such a situation.

Suppose that a wine of 15% alcohol is required. Six pints (3.4 litres) of must have been prepared from the ingredients; how much sugar will be needed to produce the desired level of alcohol? The hydrometer is the only way in which you can tell how much natural sugar has been extracted from the ingredients and hence how much you need to add.

TABLE 1

Method	British	Metric
(i) Check the s.g. of the must. Suppose this is:	1.030	1.030
(ii) Refer to Table 2. This shows that s.g. 1.030 equals:	13¼ oz of sugar in 1 gallon	376 g in 4.5 litres
(iii) Adjust this figure to give the weight of sugar in 6 pints or 3.4 litres of must:	$^6/_8 \times 13¼ = 10$ oz	$^{3.4}/_{4.5} \times 376 = 284$ g
(iv) Refer to Table 2. Check the weight of sugar required for a wine of 15% (14.9%) alcohol:	2 lb 15 oz per gallon	1332 per 4.5 litres
(v) Subtract the weight of sugar already present in the must: to determine the amount to be added:	10 oz 2 lb 5 oz	284 g 1048 g

TABLE 2
HYDROMETER CHART

Specific gravity	Amount of sugar in*		Potential alcohol (% by volume)
	1 gallon lb oz	4.5 litres grams	
1.010	4¾	135	0.4
1.015	7	198	1.2
1.020	9	255	2.0
1.025	11½	326	2.8
1.030	13¼	376	3.6
1.035	15½	439	4.3
1.040	1 1½	496	5.1
1.045	1 3½	553	5.8
1.050	1 5½	610	6.5
1.055	1 7¾	673	7.2
1.060	1 9¾	730	7.9
1.065	1 11¾	787	8.6
1.070	1 14	851	9.3
1.075	2 0	907	10.0
1.080	2 2½	978	10.6
1.085	2 4½	1035	11.3
1.090	2 6½	1091	12.0
1.095	2 8¾	1155	12.7
1.100	2 10¾	1212	13.4
1.105	2 12¾	1269	14.2
1.110	2 15	1332	14.9
1.115	3 1	1389	15.6
1.120	3 3¼	1453	16.3
1.125	3 5¼	1510	17.1
1.130	3 7½	1573	17.8
1.135	3 9½	1630	18.5
1.140	3 11¾	1694	19.3

*Remember that these figures refer to the amount of sugar dissolved in a must to give a total volume of one gallon or 4.5 litres. They do *not* refer to the amount of sugar *added* to one gallon (4.5 litres) of liquid.

This information is reproduced from Boots product literature, by kind permission of The Boots Company PLC.

TABLE 3
HYDROMETER CHART FOR AMERICAN READERS

This chart takes account of the smaller volume of the United States gallon, and should not be confused with the chart giving British and Metric measurements on page 00.

Specific Gravity	Amount of sugar in 1 US gallon		Potential alcohol (% by volume)
	lb	oz	
1.010		4	1.4
1.015		6	2.0
1.020		8	2.8
1.025		9	3.4
1.030		11	4.1
1.035		13	4.8
1.040		15	5.5
1.045	1	0	6.2
1.050	1	2	6.9
1.055	1	4	7.6
1.060	1	6	8.2
1.065	1	7	8.9
1.070	1	9	9.5
1.075	1	10	10.2
1.080	1	12	11.0
1.085	1	14	11.6
1.090	2	0	12.3
1.095	2	2	13.0
1.100	2	4	13.6
1.105	2	5	14.4
1.110	2	7	15.0
1.115	2	9	15.7
1.120	2	11	16.4

Gravity and Specific Gravity

Some authors write about "gravity" rather than specific gravity. In fact the word gravity just refers to those figures of the specific gravity reading which fall after the decimal point. Thus, for example, s.g. 1.020 becomes gravity 20; s.g. 1.115 becomes gravity 115. For specific gravities less than 1.000, the gravity becomes negative: for example, s.g. 0.995 equals gravity −5.

Measurement Conversion Information

TO CONVERT	FROM	TO	
	Pounds	Kilograms	Multiply by 0.45
	Kilograms	Pounds	Multiply by 2.2
	Ounces	Grams	Multiply by 28
	Grams	Ounces	Multiply by 0.035
	Fl oz (British)	Millilitres	Multiply by 28.4
	Ml	Fl oz	Multiply by 0.035
	Pints (British)	Litres	Multiply by 0.57
	Litres	Pints	Multiply by 1.75
	Gallons (British)	Litres	Multiply by 4.55
	Litres	Gallons	Multiply by 0.22
	Fahrenheit	Centigrade	Subtact 32 then Multiply by 0.55
	Centigrade	Fahrenheit	Multiply by 1.8 then add 32

A Note for American Readers

Not all the fruits and plants mentioned in this book will be familiar to American winemakers, so this section contains a few notes which may help to overcome any problems in this respect. Of course American readers will be able to take full advantage of their native plants to create new recipes according to their own tastes and preferences. Here, though, are some explanations of names you may not have come across.

Bilberry or blueberry

Both these plants belong to the same family. The British bilberry — which is also known as the blaeberry or whinberry — goes by the technical name of *Vaccinium myrtillus*; the American blueberry is a close relative called *Vaccinium corybosum*. (There are some other types, but these are the most common.) The difference between them lies mainly in the fact that the bilberry grows wild in the acid moorlands of Britain, whereas the blueberry is carefully cultivated in America. The recipes in this book for bilberry wine can be used with either bilberries or blueberries.

By the way, another common member of the *Vaccinium*

family is the cranberry. Although I've never used this fruit as an ingredient, it may be worth substituting cranberries in one of the bilberry recipes.

Plums, greengages, bullaces and damsons

The European plum comes in many forms. Most Americans probably think of it as a blue-skinned fruit with yellow pulp, but there are also red- and green-skinned varieties. The green-skinned variety is known as the Greengage in England. It is probably the sweetest type of plum, and worth growing if you can get hold of it. Another good fruit is the hybrid produced by crossing the Japanese plum with the native American Sand Cherry. This hybrid is known as the "Bush Cherry" and comes in many varieties, such as Compass, Red Diamond and Oka.

The bullace and damson are small, wild European plums, common in the English countryside. They are small and sour when raw, suitable only for cooking and winemaking. Perhaps the nearest American equivalent is the chokecherry (*Padus virginiana*) which, like the damson, has a dark colour and is thought of as a well-flavoured cooking fruit. It should be eminently suitable for winemaking, but do remember the *leaves* are poisonous.

Cherries — sweet and sour

As with many fruits, the "sour" or "cooking" varieties of cherry are often more suitable for winemaking than the sweet, because they have a higher level of acidity. The European Morello Cherry is a rather sour variety (although it can be eaten raw); the nearest US equivalent is the sour cherry *Prunus cerasus*, of which the hardiest variety is called "Northstar".

Another American cherry worth trying is the sweet and sour hybrid known as the Duke Cherry. However, sweet cherries — particularly Bing cherries — would probably not make an outstanding wine unless they were mixed with some sour cherries.

Apples

Apples, so it is claimed, are America's most popular temperate zone fruit. Certainly the apple is one of our most versatile fruits, for there is a variety suited to every purpose: for desserts, cooking, cider, wine, or sauce. The best apples for winemaking are those which are best for cooking. In England this includes the famous Bramley; but no matter where you live, any good local cooking variety can be used instead. However, if you have a dessert-apple tree and you want to use its fruit for winemaking, it is a good idea to add quite a lot of cooking or crab apples to increase the acidity of the must.

Grapes and raisins

Wine can be made, with varying degrees of success, from almost any variety of grape, but obviously the varieties specially evolved for winemaking will produce the best results. In fact the derivatives of the European vine (*Vitis vinifera*) are most suitable. There are many varieties available, but some common ones which you may care to try are: De Chaunac, Foch, Chambourcin and Bacon Noir (all red); Seyval, Cataurba and Delaware (all white). Grapes of the Muscadine vine (*Vitis roundifolia*) produce a distinctive wine with an attractive bouquet, and commonly features as Muscat or Muscatel raisins in home-wine recipes. It is worth noting that nearly all "American" grape varieties produce a wine with a distinctive flavour which, although a part of American tradition, would perhaps be considered unconventional by most Europeans. However, possibly because of the growing knowledge of European wines in the United States, there is a move to plant European vines for winemaking. If you want to experiment, and can get hold of them, it is worth trying the following varieties: Chardonnay, Sauvignon Blanc, and Riesling (white); Pinot Noir and Cabernet (red).

Herbs and Flowers

The recipe for Goldenrod wine may puzzle American readers. According to Allen Paterson, Director of the Royal Botanical Gardens in Ontario, Goldenrod is considered little more than a weed in the United States. He observes: "North American visitors seeing it cultivated in Europe are apt to fall about laughing." So although the plant is quite common on woodland edges and moorlands in Northern and Western England, I'm sorry to say US citizens may be unable to make this wine! The same is unfortunately true of the Burnet Wine. However, there are plenty of American herbs and plants suitable for flavouring wine, including, for example, jasmine, lemon balm and mint. If you do use some ideas of your own, please take care to identify the plant you are using correctly so as to avoid any danger of poisoning!

Sugar and Syrup

Apparently, golden syrup and demerara sugar are both hard to get hold of in America. Golden syrup is a partially refined form of inverted sugar syrup: demerara sugar is a granulated sugar made moist and dark by the addition of molasses. In either case, of course, ordinary sugar can be substituted. (Golden syrup contains about 20% water, so you need only add four-fifths the weight of dry sugar.) Nevertheless, American winemakers do have an advantage in the abundant supply of corn and maple syrup (which is uncommon in Britain). With the judicious use of a hydrometer, some interesting possibilities open up for adding this source of sugar to home-wine recipes. However, it may be worth trying with a single batch of wine before adding maple syrup to everything in sight, just to test the effect which it has on the flavour of the finished wine.

Index

188

Index

If you wish to learn more about home winemaking, you will enjoy reading

Home Winemaking Techniques and Recipes
by Rodney Boothroyd

If you have devised an original, prizewinning wine recipe which you would like to put forward for possible inclusion in the next edition of this book, please write to Rodney Boothroyd, c/o Allison and Busby, W. H. Allen & Co. Plc, Sekforde House, 175/9 St John Street, London EC1V 4LL.